To Peter de Vink,

Guide,

Friend,

Adventurer

and

Entrepreneurial

Role Model,

With warmest affection

enscribed.

Marco van Grondelle

THE ISMAILIS IN THE COLONIAL ERA

MARC VAN GRONDELLE

The Ismailis in the Colonial Era

Modernity, Empire and Islam

HURST AND COMPANY, LONDON

First published in the United Kingdom in 2009 by
C. Hurst & Co. (Publishers) Ltd.,
41 Great Russell Street, London, WC1B 3PL
© Marc van Grondelle 2009
Foreword © Faisal Devji 2009
Preface © J.J.G. Janssen 2009
All rights reserved
Printed in India

The right of Marc van Grondelle to be identified as the author of this publication is asserted by him in accordance with the Copyright, Designs and Patents Act, 1988.

A Cataloguing-in-Publication data record for this book is available from the British Library.

ISBN: 978-1-85065-982-2

www.hurstpub.co.uk

CONTENTS

CONTENTS

FOREWORD

Johannes J.G. Jansen

In the early 2000s Marc van Grondelle MSc devised the grandiose plan to draw a map of Islamic London. The plan was as ambitious as it was naive. If such a map had been realised, it would have been an important contribution perhaps not to Islamic Studies in the traditional meaning of that word but certainly to what may perhaps be called Islamography.

However, in the course of his work he stumbled upon a variety of archival sources concerning the relationship between the British Government and the Agha Khans, the leaders of the Ismaili movement. Perhaps these archives are not complete; perhaps parts of them are still secret. Nevertheless they are of great importance to Islamic scholarship—if only because it is not to be excluded that similar archives with similar material about other Islamic movements exist, in London, Washington and elsewhere. If so, such material has to be exploited as soon as possible.

Marc van Grondelle has reworked his Utrecht University Islamic Studies PhD into the present book. Its readers will get a surprisingly frank view into the inner workings of the former British imperial bureaucracy, and, even more importantly, they will be rewarded with a number of unexpected insights into how to conduct diplomacy when relations with potentially disruptive religious movements are at stake.

By writing this book, Dr Marc van Grondelle has made an important contribution to Islamography.

Dr Johannes J.G. Jansen   *University of Utrecht*
Houtsma Professor of Islamic Thought

PREFACE

Faisal Devji

This is a book about liberal Islam and its contradictions, one whose argument goes a long way towards transforming the scholarly and political debate about modernity in the Muslim world. Written as a diplomatic history of the relations between the British Empire and a Shiite community now dispersed across five continents, Marc van Grondelle's book provides the background for contemporary efforts by Western governments to foster "moderate" Islam at home and abroad. But at the same time it also points out the limitations of such exercises, by demonstrating how even an imperial state of Britain's calibre was finally unable to control a small and politically unimportant group like the Ismailis. And yet the result of this fascinating and ambiguous relationship was the development of liberal Islam in a form quite different from that imagined by intellectuals and policymakers today.

Liberal Muslims are often opposed to fundamentalist or "extremist" ones by their renunciation of religious authority, or at least its banishment from their politics and practices of public life. Seen as hothouse plants grown in the shadow of secular dictatorships in Asia and Africa, or as immigrants within the democracies of Europe and North America, these men and women are meant to have little influence over the politics of their more devout co-religionists. Van Grondelle's narrative, however, looks at the way in which liberal attitudes were promoted among a community of Muslims within the British Empire by augmenting the absolute authority of their hereditary religious leaders, and without the need for state-sponsored reforms or other measures of political control. My aim in this preface is to describe the context of this transformation and thus provide a broad historical setting for the book.

A venerable Shiite sect whose centres of population were historically scattered over parts of South and Central Asia as well as in the Middle East, the Ismailis have since the nineteenth century also formed migrant communities in equatorial Africa, and more recently in Western Europe and North America. Known as the Khojas, the most important group of Ismailis under British rule had its home in India, though it was to be found as a trading caste elsewhere in the Empire. Led by a growing number of prosperous merchants with interests across the Arabian Sea and Indian Ocean, the Khojas were from the late nineteenth century gradually placed under the authority of a religious leader called an Imam, thus becoming one of the many communities to be administered according to the colonial policy of indirect rule.[1] But this also meant that they were increasingly defined as a religious rather than ethnic or mercantile group, eventually to become part of an international brotherhood of Muslims.

The first Aga Khan, as the Ismaili Imam was called, had come to India in the middle of the nineteenth century as a princely refugee from Iran, where he had unsuccessfully tried to take the throne from his kinsman the Shah.[2] Having been forced to relinquish his political ambitions by the British, whose help he had initially sought, the Aga Khan turned his attention from raising money for his Persian battles among the Khojas to establishing his authority over them. The Bombay High Court decided upon the disputes over community property and customary law that resulted between the Imam and his wealthy followers by handing absolute authority over both to the former. Indeed the Aga Khan was recognised by the court as the Imam of the Ismailis in a way he had not earlier been among the Khojas, by reference to a history of which they were ignorant. Medieval texts in Arabic and Persian as well as European scholarship on Islam were deployed to create a theologically "correct" picture of Ismailism to which the Imam's Indian followers had to conform.[3]

As part of the colonial "invention of tradition", the word "Ismaili", which had hitherto existed only in specialised texts like Sunni accounts of heresy, and certainly not among the Khojas themselves, suddenly became a proper name to which ordinary people answered. In his memoirs the third and most important of the Aga Khans, whose reign began in the nineteenth century and ended in the middle of the twentieth, even went so far as to demonstrate his legitimacy by referencing a Bombay High Court judgement of 1866 rather than to any religious text, thus very clearly anchoring his own authority in colonial law.[4] It was this authority that was subsequently expanded to Ismaili communities outside India and the Empire, surviving the latter's extinction to flourish into our own times. For whether it was the law of British India or that of any other country in which they lived, the Imams have since then counselled Ismailis to live in accordance with it, as is only natural for a minority population.

After his struggle with the Khoja merchants and their clients, many of whom ended up converting to a rival Shia sect without however abandoning their name or identity as a closed trading group, the Imam consolidated his authority by "representing" the social and economic interests of the newly minted Ismailis who remained his followers. The Aga Khan could do this because his reputation as the leader of uncounted devotees spread across the world's most sensitive geopolitical fault lines made him an influential figure for the British. This source of influence was recognised and vastly exaggerated, with the Ismailis often claimed to number as many as twenty million, when their real number was probably three or four at most.[5] More than this invisible following, it was the Imam's wealth and increasingly Westernised ways that made him a good Muslim interlocutor for the Empire, and therefore a good negotiator for his community as well.[6]

In addition to representing his followers' interests in the Raj, the third Aga Khan began a process of community development by transferring wealth from the rich to the poor through charitable and other institutions concerned with health, education, housing, banking and insurance that were nevertheless controlled by wealthy Khojas, whose second sons were increasingly turning into bureaucrats in the service of their Imam. While the immediate models for such development are to be found among Quakers in England as well as Parsis in India, the Imam, much like the Pope whose status fascinated him, served as the medium through which wealth was transferred from one set of people to another. In the reign of the fourth and present Aga Khan, who acceded to the position in 1957, this initiative has been expanded into an extensive development network operating for the benefit of Ismailis and their neighbours in many parts of the world.[7]

Extraordinary about the project of development among Ismailis is the dominant position it has achieved within the community, transforming or even replacing properly religious ideals and practices with its language of improvement. Khoja institutions like prayer halls, shrines and the local religious figures controlling them, were quickly outnumbered by a development bureaucracy, which sometimes ended up marginalizing if not eliminating its predecessors. Thus hereditary leaders and saintly men whose authority did not depend upon the Imam, were replaced by a new bureaucratic elite, one that was drawn from the Khoja merchant aristocracy but possessed no constituency of its own. This new leadership of the laity continues to expand its reach and membership, as the collapse of the Soviet Union and changes of regime in places like Afghanistan have brought hitherto cloistered populations, called "emerging *jamaats*" or congregations into the fold, much like the emerging markets their countries had already become for Western capital.

All this has only accentuated the Imamate's state-like form, given its efforts to standardise Ismaili practices globally as if in a nation-state, claim ambassadorial status for the Imam's representatives in parts of Asia, Africa and even Europe or North America, and lend the Aga Khan the perquisites of a head of state by having him sign protocols of cooperation with kings, presidents and prime ministers. Indeed the community has its own constitution, flag and even, in the case of the Khojas, an anthem. So it is no wonder that in some quarters where they are disliked, Ismailis are, ludicrously suspected of trying to alter the borders of Pakistan, Afghanistan and Tajikistan and set up a state for their co-religionists who inhabit the region. More interesting than the geography of this would-be country, however, is the "invisible state" made possible by Ismaili institutions. How did such a state come into being as the imagined home of a trans-national community?

Although Ismailis were first cast in the mould of a liberal society in British India, it was in East Africa that they were turned into perhaps the most successful example of Muslim development.[8] Asian migrants who were removed from their societies of origin, rendered manageable by their smaller numbers and more cohesive by their engagement in trade, Khojas under British, German, Portuguese and Belgian rule in Africa were urged by the Aga Khans to adopt European habits in order to secure their social and economic advancement.[9] These habits included some kind of European dress for men and women, new forms of housing and hygiene as well as the use of the English language and participation in colonial education more generally. The "de-cultured" and increasingly wealthy community thus created soon became an agent of change among Ismailis in different parts of Asia.

Having migrated in large numbers to the West following decolonization in the 1960s, Khojas from East and Central Africa now provide the foot soldiers for Ismaili development projects in Pakistan, Afghanistan, Tajikistan and elsewhere. In the process these young men and women have taken the place of the European administrators to whom their fathers had looked for guidance in the past, not least because it is they who now represent Western civilization to their benighted brethren. Indeed my own experience with such projects in South and Central Asia brought home to me their resemblance to colonial forms of philanthropy, whose racial script was especially clear in situations where the darker-skinned Khojas found themselves in charge of people lighter than themselves, thus reversing the role of their former masters in a pleasing irony. Naturally there is no little ethnic tension between these apostles of progress and the needy people among whom they work.

While the Aga Khan continues to mediate a new transfer of funds between the Khojas and their co-religionists in different parts of Asia, as well as to arbitrate ethnic conflict between these groups, the wealth and international status that bolsters his leadership and allows him to play this role still depends on the old British policy of indirect rule. Except this time it is not some government but the Imam himself who promotes indirect rule in offering his services to weak and impoverished states by taking over a number of their responsibilities in the fields of health, education, agriculture and even transportation infrastructure. Generally provided in areas with large Ismaili populations, these services allow the Aga Khan some say in their governance, while offering the states concerned a guarantee of the political neutrality and even the loyalty of Ismailis. But this policy can only be temporary, depending as it does on the poverty of such governments and their Ismaili citizens. It will be difficult to prevent the politicization of Ismailis who form regional majorities in these countries and who thus cannot be managed in the same way as Khoja minorities are.

In the rich countries of the West where the Khojas are now concentrated, the philanthropy and advocacy that had once lain at the root of the Aga Khan's authority matter less and less. As a consequence Ismaili loyalty is in search of other foundations, such as charismatic forms of religion in which the Imam like the Pope or the Dalai Lama is seen

simultaneously as saint and celebrity. Indeed the steady bureaucrat-
ization of religious life and the elimination of intermediate forms of
charismatic authority among them have resulted in the development of
cults that profess loyalty to the Imam while disregarding his institutions. Led by charismatic figures who claim to represent the esoteric
meaning of Ismailism, these movements are to be found in many parts
of the world, seeking to create a more intimate and informal sphere
for religion in which authority is local and immediately available,
while prayer and discussion stretch beyond the bounds officially per-
mitted them.[10]

The continuing standardization and institutionalization of Ismailism
has as its corollary the destruction of local forms of authority and
practice, and yet as the only noteworthy religious leader left in place
the Imam cannot in his very singularity function as a theological
authority to whom individuals might turn for decisions. Moreover his
ministers are all laymen and bureaucrats who are unable to speak religiously and possess only clients of their own, rather than constituen-
cies that might be locally instructed. And so despite the advice he so
frequently dispenses, the Imam has also become a media icon and
celebrity for many of his followers, rather than solely a spiritual let
alone theological authority of any traditional kind. Indeed the Aga
Khan's charisma is tied more and more to the international recognition
and honours he receives from heads of state for his cultural and development work—as a glance at any Ismaili magazine will show. How
will this charisma and authority, deservedly earned by the Aga Khan
in his own right, be transferred to a much younger and relatively
unknown successor in the future?

Marc van Grondelle describes the politics of succession that resulted
in the elevation of the present Imam, making use of hitherto unknown
sources to show how the third Aga Khan worked with the authorities
of a rapidly contracting Empire to ensure its recognition of his grandson's claims to the Imamate. Succession had always been a fraught
exercise for the maharajas and other Indian princes among whom the
Aga Khan was officially classed, not least because the British had
sometimes refused to acknowledge their designated heirs for rival and
more amenable candidates. With the independence of India and Pakistan in 1947, the British no longer posed any threat to the Imam's
plans for choosing a grandson rather than either of his own sons to
succeed him. The problem instead was how to ensure the transfer to

this successor of the princely title that had been granted the Aga Khan by a now defunct state. This desire was linked to the more important one of making sure that Britain, which still counted tens of thousands of Ismailis among her African subjects, would by recognizing a successor guarantee his claims to the loyalties, properties and tithes due the Imam.

Though Britain had presided over the accession of the current Imam, it was clear that his authority was not going to be defined by her collapsing empire. And indeed the fourth Aga Khan has had to reinvent his role as religious leader by internationalizing it through projects of cultural and economic development in the Muslim world and beyond. This role situates the Imam as a friendly figure in the Asian and African countries where Ismailis may be vulnerable minorities, while at the same time presenting him as the face of liberal Islam in the West. And yet the colonial policy of indirect rule still remains the mainstay of Ismaili politics, deployed though it now is by the Aga Khan himself and representing in some way the continuing influence of the Raj. The delicate balance which the Imam has had to strike over the last half-century has been largely a successful one, though on occasion his good relations with the likes of the Shah of Iran or Pakistan's President Musharraf has reflected badly upon his followers after their overthrow. Sometimes the very visibility of the Imam as an urbane European becomes a sign of his community's politically quiescent and pro-Western character in the eyes of other Muslims.

The Ismailis and their Imam have managed to survive the British Empire, which gave them, like so many other Muslim, Hindu and other groups, a legal and institutional form. Indeed the Empire can even be said to survive in such communities, not only because of their continued reliance upon policies like indirect rule, but also in the fact that it is now the Aga Khan, living as he does in Europe, who represents the civilizing ideal of imperialism in the "progressive" authority he commands among followers in Asia and Africa. But do the Ismailis continue to represent a model of liberal Islam for others? Quite apart from the sectarian differences that prevent this small minority from becoming a reference point for Muslim majorities, it is not clear that the highly centralised and bureaucratized forms of governance favoured by the community and its development projects will retain their productivity in future, despite the truly remarkable work they have accomplished in the past.

The state-like forms of Ismaili governance not only appear old-fashioned in a trans-national community, they are also bureaucratic and unwieldy. Though comparative statistics are unavailable, it is probably true that the Khojas who disavowed the Aga Khan at the beginning of the last century are not less wealthy, healthy or educated than their Ismaili relatives, to say nothing of being less liberal as Muslims. They are also involved in philanthropic projects among Shiites worldwide, but without possessing even a fraction of the institutional apparatus that is characteristic of the Ismailis. The same goes for comparable Muslim communities like the Memons or Bohras, all trading groups with whom the Khojas live cheek by jowl in many parts of the world. Even within the Aga Khan's fold there exists ethnic groups like the Indian Momnas, who run their own international networks of governance and charity outside the official bureaucracy of Ismailism. And this is to say nothing of the cults that increasingly operate within the Imam's institutional domain. In other words the institutional history of the Khojas does not provide the only or even the most effective model of success for liberal Islam.

Is it possible that Ismaili religious and economic life is slowly ebbing away from the community's institutions? Whatever the case, it is the massive development projects in Asia and Africa that today seem to provide these institutions with their legitimacy, offering in the process employment and mobility to a Khoja elite now based largely in the West. The class and ethnic tensions produced by this international order, allayed though they might be by the Aga Khan's charisma and his transfer of wealth from the rich to the poor, will sooner or later come to a head, especially in areas where Ismailis form majorities comprising classes and occupations of all kinds. Unlike the Khojas who constitute a minority dominated by traders and professionals, these Central Asian populations are not only internally divided like all majorities, they are also likely to abandon the trans-national model of Ismaili governance once poverty ceases to be a primary concern and a more democratic politics becomes possible in their homelands. Such a transformation may even be pre-empted by the elevation of the next Imam, which is likely to entail the relative de-centralization of authority in the Ismaili world. Another period will then begin in the history of this remarkably successful and adaptable Muslim community.

Dr Faisal Devji　　　　　　　　　　　　　　　　　　　　*April 2009*
University of Oxford

1

INTRODUCTION AND OBJECTIVES

The purpose of this book is to examine the processes and interactions that have led to the modernization and successful co-optation of a particular movement in Islam. It will do so by examining, from the perspective of the British government, the recent past of a comparatively small branch of Shi'a Islam, the Nizari Ismailis. In its present form, this Muslim community may, from a Western European perspective, be regarded as largely aligned with British interests politically, and successful in contemporary British society in social and economic terms.

The book will examine and emphasise the diplomatic interaction between the British Empire and later the British Commonwealth on the one hand, and the Nizari Ismaili movement on the other, in the period 1839 to 1969. This timeframe saw the development of the Ismailis from a small and obscure sect surrounded by ill-informed historical legend into a still small but highly organised temporal and religious movement, which was (and still is) considered a staunch ally of Britain. (The term 'movement' is defined, and the reasons for its use explained, below.) The research presented in this book seeks to answer a number of fundamental questions regarding the wider developing relationship between movements in contemporary Islam and what might conveniently be termed 'The West', in particular the democratic, Judeo-Christian societies of Western Europe and the United States of America. In these increasingly polarised times, it seeks to examine a particular example of the effective co-optation of a Muslim movement by the West (in this particular case as personified by British foreign and colonial policy) to the mutual benefit of both the movement and the British state apparatus with which it interacted.

It furthermore seeks to clarify which processes and actions have shaped such an evolving relationship, and under which social and political conditions this alignment and co-optation have taken place. It will also examine the time it took for this relation to fully mature, and some of the pitfalls which might have upset the evolving relationship. Lastly, it will draw conclusions regarding the applicability of the findings to the challenges posed by the evolving relationship between Islam and 'The West' as we experience this relationship today.

The book will draw almost exclusively on original official sources. These are made up of diplomatic and ministerial correspondence and other such documents from British official archives, a number of which have been recently released under the Freedom of Information Act. In particular, it will examine and reference documents from the British India Office, the Colonial Office, the Foreign and Commonwealth Office, the British intelligence services, the Prime Minister's Office, the Treasury, the Home Office, and a large number of diplomatic missions and legations throughout the former British Empire and Commonwealth. Where it is necessary to put these documents in context, or where it is unavoidable to contrast public statements and publications with more restricted official documents, the latter will be complemented by the published writings of the Aga Khan III, and on occasion by reference works regarding the past of the Ismaili movement or wider historical developments. Taken together, these documents shed light on the careful (mutual) cultivation of friendly relations, and gradually strengthening ties, between the Ismailis and Her Majesty's Government. This complex but interesting relationship has taken more than a century to develop and reach full maturity.

As will become clear from the material examined in this book, the Ismaili movement has, over the period under examination, undergone a remarkable transformation from a little-noticed entity which hardly stood out from its social and economic surroundings into a small but highly organised movement, clearly identifiable and distinct from its religious and socio-economic origins. This observation gave rise to the title of the book, 'Modernity, Empire and Islam', which is worthy of some elaboration.

The German-American political scientist and sociologist Karl Deutsch[1] identifies a number of key elements of modernity such as 'easy and effective communications' and a 'high degree of urbanisation'. He frequently refers to those values and behaviour, which are commonly experienced as modern, in what may best be termed 'The West', including such values as (a degree of) equality of men and women, and (a degree of) tolerance towards social, ethnic and religious minorities. It is clear from observation of and interaction with the Ismailis that all these factors apply to the contemporary Ismaili movement, and certainly to those components of the movement in its dominant centre in the United Kingdom, and presumably—though it was not directly observed—in countries such as Canada, France, Portugal and the United States with which the UK element is intimately connected.

In the sociology of change, a number of researchers argued that achieving change requires the crossing of some key 'threshold', also described as a 'tipping point', which separates the original state of the entity from the new situation. In particular, the American sociologist Granovetter and his British colleague Gladwell,[2] as well as the mathematically inclined American sociologist Hinds,[3] give attractive and workable sociological descriptions of this process of transition. Gladwell in particular formulated a workable description of key actors in the phenomenon which, as we shall see in chapter 3 of this book, fits remarkably well with the person of Aga Khan III.

Hence, based on these sociological considerations, the formula 'Modernity, Empire and Islam' can be taken as an adequate description of the transformation undergone by the Ismaili movement during the period in question, and thus provides a useful main title for this book, on the understanding that the emphasis of the research will be on actions external to the movement (i.e. actions by the British Government) and their interaction with one key agent of change within the movement, namely Aga Khan III. This emphasis is the direct result of the available source material.

With regard to the sources describing the workings of the remarkable process of modernization, the author is aware that drawing largely on British government archives presents a one-sided picture of the relations between the Ismailis and the British authorities. Yet this is precisely the purpose of the book: to describe, from a British official perspective, the gradual process of alignment, cooptation and modernization of one particular Muslim movement, and to draw conclusions from this process.

The author would have preferred to contrast this material with documents and correspondence internal to the Ismaili movement, or indeed material from the private papers and correspondence of the movement's leadership in the persons of Aga Khan III and IV, or of their closest advisers. However, such material is not readily accessible. Although members of the movement have published selected material emanating from the Ismaili leadership, this is invariably heavily edited and usually takes the form of benign policy statements in the form of selected speeches or other such publications. The hard core of reality that could be illustrated by detailed day-to-day and issue-by-issue interaction and correspondence within the movement's leadership remains inaccessible to research for the time being.

Likewise, while interactions with the Institute of Ismaili Studies, London, and other Ismaili bodies in the United Kingdom were always cordial, no active support was forthcoming for archival research regarding the period in question. Although, by contrast, active research is being conducted regarding the formative history of the Ismailis, and particularly regarding their glory days during the times of the Fatimid caliphate, abundant contact with Ismaili researchers did not lead to any access to relevant material on the more recent period of history that is the subject of this book. In a number of meetings, the author was politely reminded that the movement prefers to research and publish the early history of Ismailism, and steers away from examining the more recent past. Thus there is little material of Ismaili origin to cover the period in question, other than the semi-official and official correspondence which resides now in the British archives.

Basing the research on British official sources was therefore a deliberate choice, given the fact that no independent, reliable secondary sources exist in the public domain regarding the shaping of the Ismaili-British relationship during the chosen period. There are, of course, myriad biographies, autobiographies and indeed hagiographies from Ismaili sources, in particular of Aga Khan III who led the movement for most of the period in question. These invariably portray the movement and its leader in a favourable light. There are also a significant number of anti-Ismaili books, articles and pamphlets with the opposite tone and intention. Quite a few of these purport to be written by authors who either have been Ismailis themselves or claim to have been Ismaili to lend further credibility to their writings. A prime example of this is Meherally Akbarally's *A History of the Agakhani Ismailis*[4] in which a wide range of statements are made, purportedly by a former Ismaili, each of which is put in a wider Quranic context to emphasise the un-Islamic nature of the misdeeds allegedly committed by members of the community. It is to some extent elegantly written and argued, but does not constitute an objectively verifiable source.

Whether pro- or anti-Ismaili, and regardless from which source these writings emanate, the great majority of publications regarding the movement are clearly aimed at a wide audience with the intention of presenting a particular point of view regarding the movement, its leadership and its Islamic credentials. None of these many books and pamphlets provides us with a detached, scientifically neutral and verifiable perspective on the development of relations between Britain and the Ismailis during the period in question.

To achieve this, we must therefore consult the official archives of the East India Company and the British Government which are publicly accessible under law, and which operate under strict regulations regarding the preservation of, and access to, documentary material. Only these archives contain the verifiable written record of Britain's interaction with the Ismailis, as set out in dispassionate diplomatic, administrative and civil service correspondence which was—at the time of writing—not for public consumption. Hence, given a lack of direct access to internal Ismaili sources, it must be considered the most reliable source of information regarding British policies and the evolving relationship with the Ismaili movement during the period covered by this research. However, this is not to say that such material is an entirely neutral source. The British colonial administrators, diplomats and civil servants, as well as their political masters, played a game of their own: a game to promote British interests and to further British commercial and imperial ambitions. And since the authors are human, no doubt some of the correspondence is at least partly influenced by individual ambitions and other such emotions which were prevalent at the moment of writing.

Nonetheless, given that this material was not written for publication, and since it demonstrates the inner workings of the British Government over many decades and on a variety of issues related to the Ismaili movement, it sheds a worthwhile light on the careful mutual cultivation of relations between Britain and the Ismailis. In addition, the traditionally restrained and measured style of correspondence common among senior British officials, and the consistency of the evolving policies pursued towards the Ismailis, lend further credibility to these sources, and make them a body of information much to be preferred over writings which were destined for immediate public consumption.

The source material reveals that there has never been one single, clearly defined and articulated British government policy in dealing with the Ismaili movement and its leadership. Indeed, the sources will demonstrate that on occasions, individual officials disagreed and quarrelled as to the course of action to be taken by HM Government in a specific situation. However, the material will demonstrate that there has been a recognizable, generally applied course of action *vis-à-vis* the movement, which has found expression in the interactions between it and British officialdom.

It can be presumed that similar material is preserved in the private archives of the Aga Khans and the wider Ismaili movement, and it is to be hoped that these will one day be open to examination. As mentioned above, such material could not be accessed as part of this research, but it would shed an interesting light on the internal perceptions of British policy and behaviour within the Ismaili leadership. Since the material could not be examined, and since it falls outside the scope of this book, it must regrettably be left to future researchers to examine this particular Ismaili perspective on the development of the British-Ismaili relationship during the period in question.

In a wider sense, the book will end with a recommendation for future research and examination of British, Indian and Pakistani archives in 2014 and beyond, when (under the 50–and 100–year retention rules) these archives may quite conceivably yield further interesting material regarding the special relationship between the Ismaili Muslims and Her Majesty's Government, quite probably including some sensitive services mutually rendered in the great events shaping our time.

To put the origins of the research, and the origin of the research questions which are presented in this book, into context, it may interest the reader to know that the original aim of the research project was not to investigate the evolving relationship between Britain and the Ismailis, but to create a socio-demographic 'map' of the various Shi'a communities in London. The aim was to give such diverse information as those communities' countries of origin, demographic characteristics, forms of worship and socio-economic activities, in order to gain a better understanding of Shi'a Muslim life in London in the early twenty-first century. Alas, the unfortunate and tragic events of 7 July 2005 in London quite unexpectedly resulted in insurmountable barriers being raised against conducting such research in the climate which has subsequently grown up around (and within) the major Muslim communities in the United Kingdom. Cooperation for such work vanished overnight, and a dark cloud of distrust and suspicion was cast over the community and its interaction with the society surrounding it. However, this major setback gave rise to the question whether there were any Muslim communities left in modern London which remained to all intents and purposes integrated in British society, and if so, how this integration and alignment had come about. Was it a natural development, or was there active intervention by either of the parties? Was it a mere coincidence, or the result of sustained relationship building? And if so, by what mechanism was this relationship built, by what kind of interaction, and how quickly?

This in turn led to the realization that there exists at least one Shi'a community which, however small in number, is not only well settled in British society but is socio-economically successful, and even enjoys firm links with the British establishment. When it became clear upon close interaction and further investigation how modernised, successful and integrated this small and yet thriving community of Shi'a Muslims is today, it was but a small step to decide to investigate the processes by which this remarkable alignment between Britain and the Shi'a Imami (Nizari) Ismaili Muslims was brought about.

In undertaking this research, it is hoped to add to the ever evolving body of knowledge regarding contemporary Islamic movements, and to provide an insight into one small Shi'a movement's remarkable journey along the arduous road towards modernisation, transformation and alignment with modern Britain. A journey which appears to have been made while not only retaining the key bonds of Faith and Community, but actually strengthening these bonds and at the same time achieving socio-economic success as a strongly networked and cohesive community of the Faithful in the globalised world of the twenty-first century.

2

FROM 'ASSASSIN LEGENDS' TO MODEL CITIZENS

A BRIEF HISTORY OF THE ISMAILI MUSLIMS

Before examining the processes leading to the establishment of today's modernised and at least partly co-opted Ismaili community, it is necessary to place the movement in a historical context. This summary of Ismaili history, which is currently undergoing significant historical reinterpretation, serves only to illustrate the development of the movement, and as such provides the background for the subsequent chapters on the modernization process and Ismaili-British diplomatic interaction.[1]

First emergence of the Ismaili movement

The Ismaili movement has undergone a complex and turbulent development since it first appeared as a significant movement in Islam around the middle of the eighth century AD. Delving back into the mists of time, the few historians who have studied Ismailism have struggled to find adequate original sources regarding the early history of the movement. Indeed, it is safe to say that the first two centuries of the Ismailis' existence as an identifiable entity remain the most obscure and unexplored period of their comparatively little-known history.[2]

However, on the basis of current understanding, it may be taken for a fact that the movement has its roots in the Imami Shi'a tradition, and that it shares these roots with the Twelver Shi'a community, which is far more numerous and indeed significantly more visible and vocal today. A schism with the mainstream Imami Shi'as around the year

765 AD, following the death of Imam al-Sadiq, led to the forming of a breakaway faction, which was initially located in southern Iraq. This faction recognised the authority and claims to the Imamate of al-Sadiq's eldest son Ismail, drawing its name from him. The movement has continued to recognise the authority of his descendents as their legitimate Imam to the present day.

By the middle of the ninth century, the community appears to have expanded significantly in terms of numbers and geographical spread, and gradually developed into a (largely secret) religious movement with political aims. This movement, designated as *al-da'wa* or *al-da'wa al-hādiya* ('the rightly guiding mission'), aimed to overthrow the politically and religiously dominant Abbasid caliphate. The formal religious basis of this conflict was a doctrinal dispute over the lineage and authority of the Imams, with the Ismaili community clearly aiming to install an Ismaili Imam as overall leader of the Muslim Faith. It may be supposed that more worldly and temporal interests played a role, in addition to the purely religious ones. But whatever the ultimate drivers in this struggle, the movement is known to have dispatched a large number of *da'is* (or 'emissaries') throughout the Islamic world to spread its message. Operating secretively, and more often than not by word of mouth rather than by writing pamphlets or other religious literature, they preached a revolutionary philosophy. Revolutionary, both in religious *and* in political terms.

The Fatimid period

The Ismaili message seems to have appealed to a critical mass of followers, and brought about the establishment of the Fatimid state— perhaps more correctly referred to as the Fatimid Empire—in North Africa in 909. This geographically large and politically powerful state stretched at its height from Egypt to Sicily, and from Yemen to the Hijaz in Arabia. It controlled, for a while, Mecca and Medina, and founded Al-Azhar as a centre of learning in Cairo. And as a political and military entity, it was a state in direct and sometimes violent competition with the Abbasid caliphate, and indeed with the wider manifestations of the Sunni interpretation of Islam.

A wide variety of sources suggest that the Fatimid period may be considered the golden age of Ismailism.[3] The Ismaili interpretation of the Faith of Islam was openly celebrated within the boundaries of the

Fatimid state without fear of persecution. And a rich diversity of literature, philosophy and scientific thought seems to have found expression.

But this period in Ismaili history also triggered the publication of a veritable avalanche of literature, especially from Abbasid sources, which we would perhaps refer to as mere propaganda in today's context. In this genre of literature the Fatimid caliphate in particular, and the Ismaili interpretation of Islam as a whole, were subjected to virulent spiritual attack.[4] It is worth noting that the followers of Ismailism outside the borders of the Fatimid caliphate appear to have suffered significant persecution in this period, and were either converted back into the mainstream interpretation of Islam which was prevalent in their location or forced to resort to *taqiyya*, the precautionary concealment of belief.[5]

Around 1094, the Ismaili movement experienced a schism which led to the movement being split into the Nizari and Musta'li branches. The latter community lives on in Yemen and in India where they are known today as Bohras. The numerically larger community of Nizari Ismaili Muslims, however, formed a state centred on the fortress of Alamut in Persia, which also encompassed parts of today's Syria. Mountain strongholds seem to have been a distinguishing feature of this state, indicating uncertain times and significant political and military tensions with neighbouring rulers.[6] Nonetheless, the Ismailis managed to hold out with a considerable degree of success. However, this political and military success came at a significant price in terms of their reputation as a movement, and their place in history.

The assassin legends

As the contemporary media illustrate, the image of a social, political or religious movement is rarely shaped by cool-headed assessment, and is rarely based on dry facts. The image of the Ismailis is no exception. Modern research into the movement is increasingly demonstrating that over the centuries, the great majority of literature concerning the movement was written by political and religious opponents.[7] As mentioned earlier, this is especially true during the times of fierce competition between the Abbasid and Fatimid caliphates.

The movement's historical image as a secretive, militant and revolutionary movement was further strengthened by the Crusaders, who came into contact (and indeed into conflict) with the Nizari Ismailis in their mountain strongholds during their repeated attempts to reach, conquer and retain the Holy Land. A wide variety of medieval European sources mention the existence of an 'Old Man of the Mountain' as leader of the Ismailis. Although based on a historical figure, the leader of legend was credited with organizing a highly effective political instrument by having his own corps of ultra-loyal, deeply indoctrinated killers.[8] These were, according to myth, recruited and subsequently intoxicated with liberal doses of hashish. These young men were brought into a secret garden in one of the established Ismaili mountain fortresses and given a foretaste of paradise, after which they were sent on their deadly missions. Whether or not this is entirely factual is open to conjecture.

There were some noteworthy political assassinations at the time which were attributed to the Ismailis, including the murder of the Sunni vizier Nizam al-Mulk in 1092[9] and that of Conrad of Montferrat, king of the Latin Kingdom of Jerusalem, in 1192,[10] but it is unproven whether these were perpetrated by individuals who were indoctrinated in accordance with the myth. Nevertheless, the legend has over time given rise to a new word in the international vocabulary, because the hashish-intoxicated followers gained prominence as the '*hashishin*', which later evolved into the modern word '*assassin*' that has graced most Western European languages. The legend has grown ever stronger over the centuries, and seems to live a life of its own. No less an authority than Marco Polo reported his encounters with the movement, and reaffirmed the Assassin legend, although contemporary research indicates that he is unlikely ever to have come into contact with them.[11] Indeed, it is reasonable to assume that he added this information to the stories of his travels after his return to Italy. Moreover, modern investigations and archaeological research carried out in the Ismaili mountain strongholds have so far failed to find any evidence of a secret garden.[12]

All of this adds up to the conclusion that the Ismailis, often in the minority and struggling for survival over the centuries, seem not to have been overly preoccupied with writing their own history. Or, in more modern terms, they seem to have spent very little time 'branding' themselves for the benefit of contemporaries, or for future historians. As always, history was written by the victor, or by the establishment in later centuries, and interpreted in accordance with the necessities of the day.

Since the advent of modern Ismaili studies in the 1930s many of these legends have gradually been refuted, or have been placed in the political context of the time. Nonetheless, the stories live on, both within the overall community of Islam and within the non-Islamic world, as a quick glance on the internet will show. And this is quite understandable, since romanticised stories concerning secret societies, mysticism and assassins have much to interest the public, no less today than in previous centuries.

An Ismaili diaspora

Let us now return to the course of Ismaili history, leading to the establishment of today's worldwide community. The golden age of Nizari Ismailism came to a cruel and abrupt end around 1256, with the ferocious onslaught of the Mongol invasions which resulted in the fall of the Nizari strongholds, and indeed the end of the Nizari state.[13] There were well-recorded massacres, combined with the destruction of much of the Ismailis' infrastructure and cultural treasures, including their libraries. In fact, from that moment on, thanks to the Mongols, the Ismaili movement has experienced its own equivalent of the 'diaspora' of the Jewish people. They lived on in Syria and Yemen, in Persia and India, and indeed throughout the Middle East and South Asia. But they always lived as a minority in an environment dominated by another interpretation of the Faith, and were ruled by Twelver Shi'a, or Sunni, or in later centuries European overlords. They were often uprooted and forced to migrate in significant numbers. Some Persian Ismailis managed to flee to Central Asia and Sind in north-west India, and succeeded over the centuries in converting a significant number of indigenous people to Ismailism, thereby establishing the numerically large Khoja community of Ismailis (i.e. those Ismailis who are descended ethnically from converted Indian Hindus).

Facilitated by the existence of the British Empire and its safe seaways, there was a significant migration of these Indian Ismailis to East Africa in the nineteenth and the early twentieth century. And in the process they changed, slowly but surely, from farmers to people of commerce and trade, adapting to their new social and economical environment. And they evolved as a temporal and religious movement, once again embracing visibly centralised leadership of their Faith and community, under the leadership of their Imams, the Aga Khans. This

13

was to have a profound impact on the movement and its socio-economic success. As we shall discuss in chapter 4, the influence of Sir Sultan Mohammed Shah, Aga Khan III (1877–1957), in particular has had a profound effect, striving as he did for the modernization, organization and education of his followers, as well as centralised control over his movement, in which efforts he was actively aided and abetted by the British Empire.

As recently as the 1960s, the policies and actions of some African leaders, and the resulting racial and political turmoil they engendered, again uprooted a large segment of the Ismaili community. As we shall see in chapter 8 of this narrative, the East African Ismailis were forced to migrate, and in doing so they emigrated by language ability: from Mozambique to Portugal, from French Africa to France, and from English-speaking East Africa to Canada, the United States, and to England. Their emigration was supported in no small measure by the British Foreign and Colonial Offices. This more recent migration triggered the establishment of the contemporary Ismaili community in England.

The Ismaili community in Britain, and defining the Ismailis as a 'movement'

The Ismaili community (or *Jama'at*) in England numbers just over 10,000 members, mainly located in London. The great majority of its members are of Indian ethnicity, but of East African geographical origin. The *Jama'at* also includes a small number of Ismailis of Persian descent. Although the community does not publish membership lists or other demographic information, from my contacts with it in 2005 and 2006, the Ismaili *Jama'at* in England may best be described, using the traditional British method of social ranking, as middle class and indeed upper middle class.

Academics, doctors, lawyers, engineers and other key professionals are well represented, as are shopkeepers, traders and people of more substantial commercial backgrounds. Shaped by the forces of history, the community is not exactly secretive (except when it comes to the specific rituals of their faith, and their financial affairs), but it does not seek to share its inner workings, nor is it cooperative towards those outside the movement who seek to get closer acquainted without fully joining the Ismaili interpretation and celebration of the Faith. However, from interaction and observation, the community may certainly be described as well organised, highly disciplined, and very forward looking in its social policies and temporal activities.

When defining the movement (or more particularly those elements of the Ismaili movement resident in the United Kingdom) in the terminology associated with the sociology of religion, one is left struggling to choose between the terms 'sect' and 'cult'. In the classic definitions of Stark and Bainbridge[14] a 'sect' is defined as *a deviant religious organisation with traditional beliefs and practices*. By contrast, a 'cult' is defined as *a deviant religious organisation with novel beliefs and practices*. According to these definitions both are to be considered outside the mainstream of large-scale, established religious organizations.

The Ismailis themselves carefully avoid using such terminology. In everyday practice, the word *Jama'at* is commonly used by Ismailis to describe themselves and their wider community. In the rare case where a scientific publication[15] regarding the contemporary Nizari Ismailis has surfaced from within the *Jama'at*, the term 'community' was consistently used. And in the one known case where, in the 1970s, a degree of access was granted to a sociologist in order to investigate the inner workings of the movement, a subsequent scholarly publication[16] resulted, in which the word 'community' was consistently used to describe the subject of his research. In both cases, the choice of the term 'community' would appear logical, as it is a neat linguistic (but emotionally imperfect) translation of the term *Jama'at* so frequently employed by the Ismailis themselves, while avoiding the judgemental pitfalls usually associated with the terms 'sect' and 'cult'. However, when reverting to the classic definitions of Stark and Bainbridge, one must conclude that both these terms do in fact apply to the Nizari Ismailis in some measure.

Although undoubtedly Islamic in historic origins and self-perception, the Ismailis have introduced religious practices which deviate from those in the mainstream Sunni and Shi'a interpretations. A number of these are well documented, particularly in hostile literature. The Qur'an and Shari'a, so central to the experience of mainstream Islam, are largely considered of historic interest by contemporary Ismailis, who give greater credence to the *firman*s ('edicts') which emanate from their temporal leader and spiritual Imam, the Aga Khan.

Upon examining the religious practices, to the extent that they are known, one clearly finds grounds to use the term 'sect' or 'cult' to describe the Nizari Ismailis, because one detects a heady mix of traditional and novel beliefs and practices. Given that both traditional and novel beliefs are evident in the *Jama'at*, and that we are dealing with an organization which is clearly deviant from mainstream Islam, there is justification for using both these terms. And given that the modern, novel elements dominate, as evidenced by the emphasis on the *firmans* of the Aga Khan in daily life and religious practices, one must conclude that the word 'cult', although imperfect, is perhaps the most applicable description of the Nizari Ismaili religious experience.

However, using the term 'cult' ignores the vital observation that for the Ismailis, religious and temporal life are experienced as one, and that it is virtually impossible to be a 'sole practitioner' Ismaili. As documented by Clarke,[17] participation in the daily life of the community and surrender to the religious practices of what may be termed the 'cult' are inseparable. This presents us with a dilemma of sociological and theological nomenclature which, if ignored, risks presenting an incomplete picture of the Ismaili reality.

It is perfectly possible to be a member of a 'cult' and to lead a daily life unrelated to the practices and beliefs of this cult—one thinks of those cults embracing pagan rituals, with members leading working and family lives unrelated to the participation in the cult. It is also perfectly possible to be a member of a 'community' without embracing any of its beliefs, simply by living in a specific area amongst a dominant social group without actually participating in activities that define the collective character of this group. However, neither of these is possible for an Ismaili. For the modern Ismaili as described by Clarke,[18] temporal and religious life, social and economic life, family and married life, are all inextricably linked to participation in the overall Ismaili experience. Thus neither the word 'community' (which is in its essence entirely temporal) nor the words 'sect' and 'cult' represent a full understanding of the Ismaili reality.

Stark and Bainbridge[19] offer a broader sociological context which is of help in formulating an adequate descriptive and indicative term to describe the Ismailis. They seek to describe the nature of a religious entity in terms of the degree of tension between the entity and its social and religious environment, and state that 'it is when cults become religious movements that their environment heats up.' For the Ismailis in Britain, there is little actual tension between its British social context and the *Jama'at* as a whole. But in the wider domain of Islam, the Ismailis are subject to fierce criticism and are frequently deemed to be un-Islamic by their detractors. Thus the tension between the Ismailis and their religious surroundings, whether in Britain or abroad, is significant.

This suggests use of the term 'movement', as defined by Stark and Bainbridge, to describe the modern Ismaili *Jama'at*. Therefore, the word 'movement' will be predominantly used in the context of this book to describe the Ismailis, with all its connotations of an evolving body of people, linked through a myriad of tangible and intangible bonds, jointly undertaking a journey through time and history. Although still imperfect, the concept of a 'movement', more than any other terminology, seems most apt to describe the Ismaili reality, without leaning towards either a predominantly temporal or a predominantly religious interpretation of their existence.

Although it is outside the scope of this book, much theoretical analysis to define sociological terminology such as 'movement' (or, in this case, a 'new religious movement') has been carried out and published. A review of this literature further supports the use of the word 'movement' for the contemporary Ismaili *Jama'at*, although all researchers seem to struggle to find an adequate description for a thoroughly integrated temporal and religious experience as demonstrated by the Ismailis.

It is well documented, and becomes palpably clear upon closer acquaintance with the movement, that central authority over it rests with the current Aga Khan, His Highness Shah Karim al-Husayni, Aga Khan IV, 49th Imam of the Nizari Ismailis. A well educated, highly respected statesman, stemming from a family of professional high-profile diplomats, the Aga Khan is well connected and indeed well regarded among world leaders and royalty. In 1957 the title 'His Highness' was bestowed on him by Queen Elizabeth II. (The intricate and lengthy process leading to this decision is described below in Chapter 7 of this narrative, which deals with the diplomatic interaction surrounding his succession to the Imamate.) And it was Margaret Thatcher, who, when Prime Minister performed the official opening of the Ismaili Centre in London, located in the prestigious district of Kensington. Not every leader of a relatively small religious community would command such presence and such endorsement. There is a wealth of similar evidence of the social standing of the community, but this falls outside the scope of the present book.

The Aga Khan is the central figure in the Ismaili community, in both a spiritual and a temporal sense. For his followers, he is the one and only religious authority. In contrast to Sunni or Twelver Shi'a Islam, there is no guild of professional *imams*, *ayatollahs* or *ulama*. This constitutes a major difference, which influences not just the internal workings of the Ismaili movement, but also its wider dynamics. The Aga Khan alone directs the spiritual life, the activities and the organization of the Ismailis through his *firmans* (i.e. his 'edicts', more broadly referred to by the Ismailis themselves as 'guidance'). For the duration of his life, this guidance is a matter between him and the members of the *Jama'at*, and it is not for outsiders to review or publish these transactions. This is a matter of good manners, if nothing else. But much of the content and practical direction of these *firmans* may be deduced indirectly from the structure and actions of the community, and from the fact that the current Aga Khan was appointed by his grandfather, Aga Khan III, with the *express* purpose of continuing the spectacular process of modernization and centralization which the worldwide Ismaili movement has been, and is, undergoing.

The speeches, the letters and the messages to his *Jama'at* of the late Aga Khan III are now to some extent in the public domain.[20] A review of these shows clearly that they speak an unequivocal message of modernization, of education, and—interestingly to the modern observer of Islam—of the emancipation of women, who were and are encouraged and enabled to play a full and equal part in the life of the community. There is also an unambiguous message that Ismailis should always be striving for full practical integration into the countries and cultures in which they live. And very clear direction is given to obey the laws of the land, always and without reserve.

In contrast to the literature of other religious movements, there is almost no guidance about either physically or spiritually winning others over to the cause, and as a result there very little evidence, if any, of a drive, at least in Britain, to gain converts to Ismailism. Today, people are born into the community, or—on rare occasions—join on their own initiative. Increasingly, it seems, Ismailis in Western countries may marry outside the community and yet retain their faith.[21]

To understand the modern community, it is revealing also to review its organizational structure. There are councils and working groups to manage and organise the life and work of the *Jama'at*. These include councils to arrange religious education, to settle conflicts among the members, or to rule on such matters as divorce. There are organizations that help the migration of fellow Ismailis from conflict areas (including Afghanistan in recent years) and, uniquely, actively to manage the complex and lengthy process of successful re-education and socio-economic integration into their new homes, new jobs and the new culture of their host country. Members of the *Jama'at* are appointed to these working councils for fixed periods of time, directly by the Aga Khan, who seems to select them on merit only.

These positions are unpaid. The reward is spiritual and social, although there is some evidence of indirect economic benefit resulting from a high standing within the *Jama'at*. On an international level, there are a number of organizations, such as the Aga Khan Foundation and the Aga Khan University, with a strong focus on healthcare and education. And there are scholarly institutes, such as the Institute of Ismaili Studies in London, charged with performing historical research into Islam in its widest sense. Academically independent, and with refreshing openness, they strive to uncover historical facts about the history of the religion of Islam, and contribute to historical research.

In his engagements with the Ismailis, the author of this book found it interesting to note that the councils and institutes operate on yearly and five-yearly budget cycles, and on clearly documented and agreed programmes of activities. In that sense, today's modern Ismaili movement to some extent resembles the structure and working methods of a well-oiled multinational company, with the Aga Khan as its chief executive. Women play a full part in all this work. A mere glance at the pictures of members of the councils reveals that a significant number of the members are women. So it is perhaps accurate to compare the Ismaili community in some respect with a multinational company with an affirmative action and equal opportunities programme. But whatever the analogies, it is fair to conclude that this community works hard and functions well in a socio-economic sense.

To round off, we may refer to a great researcher into the history of the Ismailis, who stated in a recent work: 'The Nizaris have [...] passed the test of time, and they have emerged into the 20th century as a prosperous and progressive community. The experience of the modern Nizari Ismaili community [...] represents an exceptional record of achievement in the Muslim world, which is still deeply plagued by poverty, illiteracy and religious fanaticism.'[22]

Conclusions

From the material examined in chapter 2, we may conclude that the Ismailis are best described as a movement, rather than as a temporal community or a religious sect or cult. The Ismaili movement has experienced a turbulent formative history, including significant political and military conflict. As a result, migration and frequent resettlement have become a characteristic of the movement. Indeed, these have resulted in the movement coming into contact with the British Empire and forming extensive relations with Britain, which are a hallmark of its modern day existence. From these historical developments, a comparatively small but modern, well organised and socio-economically successful community has emerged in the United Kingdom.

The community may be described as thoroughly modernized, forward looking, and well-integrated into (but still identifiably distinct from) its social environment. The violent events in the early and medieval history of the Ismailis, and the mythology surrounding the movement which has subsequently grown up, appear not to have obstructed this development.

3

FIRST CONTACT
(1840–1914)

Aga Khan I and II as seen from a British Imperial Perspective

In the myriad colonial and government archives consulted during the research for this narrative, Aga Khans I and II barely receive any official mention. There are no records of any particular achievements, of noteworthy interactions with the colonial or central governments, or of any activities which made the Ismaili community stand out from the multitude of Muslims during their Imamate. It is known that Aga Khan I was born in Persia in 1800, and that he ruled over his followers until his death in 1881. He was made governor-general of Kerman by King Fateh Ali Shah of Persia, but was forced to leave his native land for exile in India upon incurring the displeasure of Fateh Ali Shah, who was also his royal kinsman.[1] This breakdown in royal relations appears to have emanated from a desire on the Aga Khan's part to carve out a temporal kingdom from Persia, a desire which triggered a range of armed, rebellious confrontations with the established rulers.

In an article dealing with the revolt, Algar[2] hints that the rebellion by Aga Khan I against his Persian overlords may have been welcomed by Britain, and may have received some limited support, but there is no evidence being produced to substantiate this, other than a mention that two cannon in the Aga Khan's armoury were 'probably of British provenance' and a suggestion that 'it may [...] have been no coincidence that the first stage of the Aga Khan's revolt came when Iranian troops were advancing on Herat in defiance of British wishes.' Perhaps so, but regrettably the official archives make no mention of any British support at this time to substantiate these claims.

The son and successor of this first Aga Khan, Aga Khan II, lived until 1884 and had a tragically short reign, succeeding his father in 1881 upon the latter's death but passing away himself just three years later.[3] What little official mention is made of British interaction with these first two Aga Khans must be found in files regarding their more illustrious descendent, Aga Khan III. A note from the Dominions Office[4] regarding the status and titles of Aga Khan III makes a brief reference to his predecessors, and the role they may have played in the service of the Empire:

The first Aga Khan who had dealings with the British was hereditary Viceroy of Kerman in the time of Fateh Ali Shah, Shah of Persia from 1797 to 1834. This Aga Khan took refuge in Kandahar in 1840 and established relations with the British during the first Afghan War. [which was fought from 1839 to 1842, MvG.] In 1844 he was given a pension of Rs 1,000 a month, which was continued to his successors, and the title of "His Highness". He died in 1881 and on the recommendation of the Government of Bombay the title [...] was continued to his son and successor Aga Ali Shah. On Aga Ali Shah's death in 1884 he was succeeded by the present Aga Khan, then a boy of eight, who was the first to be born a British subject.

And a (draft) letter[5] from the Colonial Office to the editor of *Burke's Peerage*, dated 18 September 1957, regarding the lineage of Aga Khan III, mentions that 'The grandfather of the late Aga Khan [Aga Khan III, MvG] was the first Aga Khan to establish relations with the British and in 1844 he was granted the title "His Highness" in recognition of his spiritual leadership of the Ismaili Khojas and for his life time only.'

Beyond these scant mentions, the official archives are silent. There is no reference to the nature of the first Aga Khan's relations with the British authorities, nor any specific information regarding the services he may or may not have rendered to the British cause in the first Afghan war.

Hopkirk's epic works, including *The Great Game*,[6] paint a vivid picture of the times and circumstances in which the contact was made. During this era a fierce, yet shadowy struggle took place between Imperial Russia and Britain to extend influence over the northerly approaches to India. A struggle which was fought in Afghanistan, around the Caspian, in Circassia, and in the then largely uncharted deserts and mountains north of the Indian empire. It was a struggle of repeated military confrontation, but also of secret geographical surveying missions, of long-range reconnaissance, and of individual British and Russian officers and adventurers approaching local rulers in attempts to win favour and conduct trade or negotiate treaties, the latter often only of temporary and dubious value. Bribery, intimidation, and the buying of local rulers' loyalties were a matter of course. According to Hopkirk, it is not without reason that Russian historians refer to this period of history as 'The Tournament of Shadows'.

Given his recent arrival in India prior to the Afghan war, it may be supposed that Aga Khan I had not had much time to organise his followers to render any large-scale direct support to the British. From the lack of official mention, his support can be presumed to have been fairly limited, although a much later obituary of his grandson in *The Times* mentions that he gave 'great assistance to British arms', without being specific as to what that assistance may have been.[7] In the above mentioned article, Hamid Algar describes some services which Aga Khan I may have rendered during the Afghan War and the British conquest of Sind, including the provision of a small number of cavalry and personally acting as an intermediary with local rulers. However, these claims are based on secondary sources, and are not substantiated by the official British archives.

The Persian royal origins of Aga Khan I may have been of interest to the British, and a reason for their financial assistance to him, keen as they were to enhance their influence in his native land. Was it purely a matter of public diplomacy to award a title and pension to a newly arrived refugee with royal blood, or was it an attempt to recruit a potential ally in a difficult military and political struggle? We do not know for certain, but a combination of these factors was probably at work. From the scant mention it receives in later times, it may well be supposed that the first contact between the first Aga Khan and the British was seen by the British as not much more than a minor event in the ever ongoing turmoil on the borders of the British Empire, perhaps handled by comparatively minor East India Company officials as a local affair of a temporary and speculative nature. No word of it seems to have reached London, to judge from what is in the archives.

Muslim education in India in the 1880s: the Ismailis still in obscurity

In the period from 1882 to 1888 the British government in India, and hence the India Office in London, were troubled by persistent complaints from the Indian Muslim community regarding the overall lack of success of Indian Muslims in obtaining state employment. The issue became a high-profile one, and commanded the attention of the Viceroy, who subsequently charged the Under-Secretary to the Government of India with resolving the matter. On 8 September 1888, the Under-Secretary wrote an extensive despatch[8] to the 'local governments and administrations' of British India, containing key correspondence regarding the history of the grievance, as well as a wide-ranging government census of the employment of Muslims in Indian government service and a range of policy recommendations. A few key extracts suffice to give a flavour of the political profile and the intensive nature of the government's attention to the matter:

In February 1882 a memorial was addressed to HE the late Viceroy by the National Muhammedan Association calling attention to the present decayed position of Muhammadans in India, to the causes which had, in the opinion of the memorialists, led to this decadence, and to the circumstances which, in their belief, tend to perpetuate that condition. The memorial was fully reported upon by the Local Governments and was also discussed by the Education Commission. [..] The present Viceroy feels special interest in the well-being and advancement of the Muhammadan subjects of the Crown in India.

Further down in the document we read:

From the statements of the memorialists and the whole previous discussions, it is clear that the chief drawback in the way of the advancement of the Muhammadan community in times past has been their inability or unwillingness to take full advantage of the State system of education. From the time of Warren Hastings to the present, this has been a matter of regret to the Government. The failure of the Muhammedans in certain provinces to compete on equal terms with Hindus for State employment has frequently been noted.

And this was backed up by a statement of the position of the Indian Government in the matter:

The Governor General in Council assumed that in all provinces where Muhammadans were few, and often exposed to all the disadvantages which affect a religious minority without wealth or superior influence, it would be the special care of Government to satisfy themselves that these endeavours to encourage the education of Muhammadans would be persistently maintained.

And lastly:

As regards Muhammadan endowments generally, these are almost invariably, it is believed, of a religious or quasi-religious character; and while it is impossible for Government to meddle with them [...] the enlightened Members of the Muhammadan community should bring pressure to bear upon their less-advanced co-religionists, in whose hands the funds of this description for the most part lie, to give a wise direction to their expenditure.

A lengthy correspondence with the governments of the various states in British India follows, resulting in an extensive census of the Muslim population in each state and the percentage of Muslims in government employment. For the purposes of this narrative, it is revealing that neither the lengthy correspondence nor the detailed census contained *any* mention of the Ismaili community as a separate entity among the Muslims of British India. This absence of any mention suggests that the Ismailis, at the time of this high-profile public grievance, were not an influential or particularly noteworthy community among the wider Muslim population of India. Clearly, they possessed neither 'wealth nor superior influence', nor were they or their leader particularly vocal in the matter of education. As we shall see in succeeding chapters, all this was to change rapidly in the decades to follow.

Enter Aga Khan III

According to a briefing note[9] contained in the files of the Colonial Office, the Right Honourable Sir Sultan Mahomed Shah, Aga Khan III, GCSI, GCMG, GCIE, GCVO was born in Karachi on 2 November 1877. He was 'by birth a British subject without citizenship'.

In later years, a set of Reuter's press agency telegrams[10] about the death of Aga Khan III would note that he '…was a child when he succeeded his father, Aga Khan II, in 1885. He was then taken to England, educated at Eton and finally sent to Cambridge university.' There is no mention in the official correspondence of the Colonial or India Offices at the time of who took the initiative to send Aga Khan III to be educated at Eton and subsequently at Cambridge. His family would no doubt have been a driving force, but it may be reasonably presumed that British officialdom played a role in securing him a place at these prestigious institutes, and in smoothing his transition to this new environment. Alas, the archives are silent on the matter. The note mentioned above[11] continues:

On the death of his father, Aga Ali Shah, in 1885 he was installed as Imam at the age of eight years. He married Shahzahdi Begum in 1897 and in the following year set out on his first European tour. [He was then 21 years of age, MvG] During his visit to Britain he was received in audience by Queen Victoria and knighted with the K.C.I.E. At that time he also made the acquaintance of the Prince of Wales (later to become King Edward VII) and set the foundations of a lasting friendship. He was created G.C.I.E. on King Edward's coronation in 1902 and in the following year was nominated a member of the Indian Legislative Council. In 1908 on a visit to France he married his second wife, Mlle. Theresa Magliano, and in the following year his first son, Mehdi Khan, was born. Mehdi Khan died two years later, a few months before Ali Khan was born.

The note continues with a detailed description of his services to the Empire, which we shall revisit in chapters 4 to 8 of this narrative.

As mentioned, the official British files regarding the youth of Aga Khan III regrettably do not elucidate on whose initiative his grand tour to Europe was undertaken, nor the specific reasons why he was invited to Buckingham Palace to be presented to Queen Victoria. However, it was not uncommon at the time for those native Indian princes and nobles who could afford the journey and associated expense to present themselves in London, both with the purpose of paying homage to their Queen-Empress, and in order to return to their fiefdoms with enhanced standing, able to regale their family and subjects with tales of their journey to the royal and administrative heart of the Empire. No doubt, this would have added significantly to their stature among their followers, whilst at the same time allowing British officials a thorough first-hand look at these ruling citizens, who were potentially able to exert a degree of influence on events in India, then the most highly prized asset of the British Empire.

It is unclear whether the young Aga Khan III had already been noticed as a person worthy of particular attention by British officials in India prior to his arrival in London at the age of eight, but in view of his reception it must be considered likely that, in the time-honoured fashion of the British ruling classes, a discreet yet close observation was kept as he matured throughout his education at Eton and Cambridge. Nor is it clear whether his contacts with the Prince of Wales were those of genuine friendship or were driven by political expediency alone. The archives of Buckingham Palace might yield the answer, but are not open to inspection.

What is certain, however, is that the Aga Khan's visit to London contributed in no small measure to his meteoric rise in social and political stature. In 1902 he was created a member of the Imperial Legislative Council, a semi-representative, partly symbolic, yet prestigious advisory body within the framework of the British imperial administration. He was then just twenty-five years old. In 1911, his treatment on ceremonial occasions was considered by the Government of India in connection with the Delhi Durbar:[12] 'It was decided that he should be invited to the Darbar by the Government of Bombay, the invitation being couched in the same terms as that addressed to 1st class Ruling Princes in that Presidency.' Courtesy of the colonial authorities, his formal status and rank in India had now been confirmed as on a par with the *crème de la crème* of Indian nobility.

In the first decade of the new century, the Aga Khan embarked on a high-profile career of public service, and rapidly became an influential figure in public opinion-making. A veritable avalanche of speeches and articles on a wide range of topics began to take shape around 1902, followed later by radio broadcasts,[13] and continued virtually uninterrupted throughout his long life. In his early publications, he tackled such diverse topics as *Muslim Education in India* (1902),[14] *The Finances of India* (1903–4),[15] *The True Purpose of Education* (1904),[16] *A Bill of Muslim Rights* (1906),[17] *Some Thoughts on Indian Discontent* (1907),[18] *Advice to the Muslim League*,[19] and *The Problems of the Minorities in India* (1909).[20]

Reviewing these publications, one cannot help being struck by the self-confidence with which the then Aga Khan tackled high-profile, yet often sensitive issues. He does not hesitate to project himself as a leader among Muslims, and he calls for their organization and unification in predominantly Hindu India. Nor does he hesitate to lecture his fellow Muslim leaders and show them the way to the emancipation as well as social and moral elevation of their followers. And he tackles Indian domestic policy, setting out his views on issues which were potentially painful to the imperial authorities, such as inter-communal strife between Hindu and Muslim. The best example of this latter genre may be found in a speech[21] delivered in 1913, protesting against the poor treatment of Indians in South Africa:

As the chairman of this public meeting, it falls to my lot to echo the feelings of the people of India which the calamities that have lately occurred in South Africa have evoked throughout the length and breath of this empire. It is no exaggeration to say that in the modern history of India, it is impossible to find a parallel to the intensity of feeling to which Indians have been stirred. [...] The controversy of the rights of the Jew formed the subject of a memorable debate in the House of Commons, when Lord Palmerstone contended that even the poorest man who bore the name of a British subject should be protected by the whole strength of England against the oppression of a Foreign Government. [...] the British subject of whatever creed or colour must be protected by the British Government from violence to his person and property wherever he went. [...] Public opinion in India cannot believe the statement that the imperial Government is helpless in the matter....

Stirring and controversial words. But they were to be the exception to the rule in his public writings. On closer inspection, one notices in the great majority of the Aga Khan's speeches and publications personal loyalty to the Empire and to the Queen-Empress Victoria (and subsequently to the King-Emperors), calls for cooperation, a de-escalating choice of words, and subtle drawing of attention to the many benefits brought by British colonial rule to backward, downtrodden India. Here it becomes clear what a happy marriage existed between the young, intelligent, eloquent and highly talented Indian-born noble with European tastes and the British Imperial government. On the one hand was a landless, energetic and impressionable young man looking for an outlet for his enormous energy, with a keen wish to centralise and modernise his followers, and with a strong desire to acquire the approval of the Queen Empress and her government. On the other hand, we see an Imperial government looking for a modern and moderate Muslim leader who would be certain to align his views largely with those of Her Majesty's government in London as it dealt with the trials and tribulations of running the Empire.

In strict sociological terms as defined by Gladwell,[22] it is clear that the Aga Khan may be described as a combination of the three types of people who are essential in producing change (a phenomenon amusingly described by Gladwell as a 'social epidemic'). Aga Khan III was certainly a *connector*, with a wide social circle, and a 'hub' of the human social network; a *maven*, also described as a knowledgeable or well informed person; and a *salesman*, able to articulate and disseminate his message in an attractive manner to a selected audience. The combination of these characteristics in one individual is unusual, and would have made the Aga Khan valuable in the eyes of the British authorities. The careful nurturing of these characteristics through British education, and through connection with key British institutions and points of view, produced for the British Empire in times of both war and peace a valuable asset who personally stood to gain from this alliance in terms of influence and temporal status, and was thereby better able to exert temporal and spiritual influence over his followers.

From the official archives, we cannot be certain which colonial civil or military servant first spotted Aga Khan III among the myriad Indian princes and nobles as a potentially valuable ally of Britain. But as we shall see in subsequent chapters, it was a talent well spotted indeed. The early efforts to introduce into Aga Khan III a spirit of unswerving love for and loyalty to Britain would be handsomely rewarded in times of great crisis, to mutual benefit.

Conclusions

From the material examined in chapter 3, we may draw the conclusion that Aga Khan I and II were known to the British authorities, but do not seem to have made a particularly noteworthy contribution to the British imperial cause. Neither was the Ismaili community in India in the 1880s noted for any particular prowess in the field of education, or singled out for particular mention in one of the great controversies surrounding the Muslims in India. Thus it must follow that the Ismaili community in India in the 1880s did not stand out in terms of particular wealth or influence compared to the overall Muslim population.

However, the standing of the community rapidly changed in the decades to follow. Aga Khan III was educated at Eton and Cambridge, which instilled in him from an early age a close personal acquaintance with England and English institutions. He was subsequently introduced to the Royal Court in London at an early and impressionable age, and active measures were taken, including the bestowing of high public honours, to cement his bond with the Crown.

Subsequently, the Aga Khan set out upon a career of public service, spreading a message of both modernization and loyalty to the British Empire among his followers as well as to a wider colonial audience. In sociological terms, Aga Khan III was thereby perfectly placed to guide the rapid transformation and modernization of the Ismaili movement.

The British authorities carefully nurtured and fostered these characteristics, and equipped him with the necessary status and information. They subsequently made use of these characteristics in Aga Khan III, thereby co-opting him and the wider Ismaili movement for the British cause and policies, to mutual benefit.

4

CRISIS YEARS

'MUCH VALUABLE SERVICE'
(1914–1920)

Prelude to War

The coming of the First World War was foreseen by many of the key politicians, publicists and analysts in the latter decades of the nineteenth century. The emergence of a strong, vibrant German empire, and the development of a powerful German navy, constituted an emerging threat to the British Empire and its lifelines. At the same time, the myriad local conflicts and dubious alliances between the unstable countries of central Europe gave rise to a new nervousness in England about the future of Europe and the British Empire.[1] Consequently, both public political debate and secret diplomatic and intelligence activity gradually prepared for the coming Armageddon. In this the British predictably made use of their extensive network of leading figures to best effect, and the Aga Khan was to play a key role.

Turkey and the Onset of War

It was well appreciated among the future belligerents, as they gradually yet inexorably divided into opposing camps, that the question of Turkey's choice of allegiance would have a profound effect on the political landscape of Europe and Asia, and on the course of the coming war. And as a result, both sides made vigorous attempts to secure Turkey's cooperation. As early as 1898, Kaiser Wilhelm II paid a state visit to the East, which turned out to be 'more of a triumphal progress. In the Ottoman capital, the Sultan's only friend was given a lavish and flattering welcome, exceeding anything previously accorded a foreign visitor'.[2] There was talk of a railway linking Berlin to the Persian Gulf. And there were bold, audacious and indeed inflammatory speeches from the Kaiser, appealing to the hearts and minds of Muslims everywhere: 'His Majesty the Sultan, and the 300 million Muslims scattered across the globe who revere him as their Caliph, can rest assured that the German Emperor is, and will at all times remain, their friend.' Such recognition of the Sultan's authority over *all* Muslims must have been most welcome to many members of the Turkish ruling elite.

The strategic implications were well understood in London too. And as part of the overall British diplomatic effort, the Aga Khan went into print,[3] outlining his personal views while taking the liberty to speak for the Indian Muslim community as a whole in doing so:

Let there be no misunderstanding of the real attitude of the Indian Mahommedan opinion towards Turkey. There is much discussion in Europe of the position of the Sultan as Khalif. The Indian Moslem does not recognise the Sultan as Khalif, and offers him no allegiance in that capacity. But he does look upon Turkey as the embodiment of the temporal power of Islam. [...] The events of the last two years have not shaken the conviction of Indian Moslems that Great Britain in her own interest should be the friend and supporter of the Ottoman power. [...] The Indian Moslem does not ask for the surrender of the British interests; he simply points out that these interests are in accord with Moslem sentiment and wishes.

Here we clearly see the Aga Khan in the role which he had gradually shaped for himself, and which had gradually been shaped for him by Britain: an intelligent, articulate, yet moderate figurehead on behalf of Muslim interests in India. He frequently produced publications which were sometimes mildly critical, more often than not very illuminating, but which always took care to express a deeply felt loyalty to the Empire, and demonstrated the Aga Khan's willingness to come to Britain's aid in a crisis.

It would later be mentioned in his obituary, issued by Reuters,[4] that 'during the first world war, the Aga Khan assisted the allied cause when the Kaiser tried to foment a holy war by suggesting the allies were attacking the holy place of Islam.' A short mention in a lengthy obituary, yet a crucial episode for the British Empire and as a result, for the future of the Ismaili movement.

A Call to Arms

Upon the outbreak of the First World War, the Aga Khan busied himself with support for the war effort, demonstrating his personal commitment to diplomacy and to support in a more direct sense. It is reported in the archives[5] that he immediately cabled the *Jama'ats* of his followers stressing the obligation to remain loyal to the British Crown. This message could not be recovered as part of the research for this narrative, but it must be considered more than likely that it was indeed despatched.

Addressing volunteers for the Indian Field Ambulance Corps[6] in October 1914, the Aga Khan linked their efforts without hesitation to the cause of Empire:

I am unable to tell you the feelings of pride and joy with which I address my fellow countrymen here whose spontaneous desire to actively serve the King-Emperor in this supreme hour in the destinies of Europe and the Empire has found action in the formation of the Indian Field Ambulance Corps. [...] You represent a spirit which is universal amongst our countrymen in India and here. [...] That spirit of patriotism finds expression in the intimation of your committee to the India Office placing your services unconditionally at the disposal of the authorities, as a proof of India's desire to share the responsibilities, no less than the privileges, of membership of this great Empire.

Amusingly, after heaping praise upon the volunteers and extolling the virtues of Empire, the Aga Khan then goes on to berate the Chancellor of the Exchequer, David Lloyd George, in the same speech:

Representations made to me from many quarters [...] showed that Moslem sensibilities have been deeply wounded by an observation Mr Lloyd George let fall in the otherwise inspired and splendid recruiting speech he delivered in London on the 19th September. The just scorn and ridicule that he poured upon the blasphemous claims of the Kaiser to be the weapon and the sword of the Almighty was followed by an unhappy and an unfortunate comparison that there has been nothing like it since the days of Mahomet.

And indeed, a most unhappy remark[7] had been made by Lloyd George (then Chancellor of the Exchequer, later to be Prime Minister) during a patriotic meeting on 19 September 1914, in the Queen's Hall in London:

You saw that remarkable speech which appeared [...] this week. It is a very remarkable product, as an illustration of the spirit we have got to fight. It is his speech to his soldiers on the way to the front: "Remember that we German people are the chosen of God. On me, on me as German Emperor, the Spirit of God has descended. I am His weapon, His sword, and His vizard! Woe to the disobedient! Death to cowards and unbelievers!" There has been nothing like it since Mahomet. Lunacy is always distressing, but sometimes it is dangerous, and when you get it manifested in the head of the State, and it has become the policy of a great Empire, it is about time when that should be ruthlessly put away.

However, the Aga Khan quickly defused the controversy in his subsequent speech: 'It is however my belief and conviction that the observation coming from one who has never lived outside this country, or in contact with Moslem people, was, so to speak, an unconscious sort of passing reference not really meant towards the Prophet of Islam personally. I am sure it was not meant to be offensive and was unpremeditated.'

Thus, by drawing attention to the issue whilst immediately defusing the controversy which resulted, the Aga Khan skilfully manoeuvred to strengthen his credentials both as a Muslim leader and as a friend of Empire to whom those in authority would have reason to be grateful.

And a call to the purse—a conversation with Austen Chamberlain

The Aga Khan did considerably more than call for active personal and military support for the British cause in the Great War. The official archives contain a comparatively small file[8] from 1915 which is marked 'Closed Until 1966', an unusually long period which indicates that both the officials concerned and the Aga Khan must have considered it likely that the contents of the file would displease various parties if released any earlier. It refers to a conversation between the Aga Khan and the Rt. Hon. Austen Chamberlain, half-brother to the future Prime Minister and then Secretary of State for India. A memorandum[9] describes the conversation:

The Aga Khan came to see me this afternoon by appointment. [...] under present circumstances, he wished to direct my attention to the possible participation of India in the Loans required to finance the war. He said that, speaking privately, it must be remarked that financially India was doing less than her proportion, inasmuch as the expenses of her troops in the field were borne by this country [Britain, MvG] and he felt that she both could, and ought to, take her share in providing the money for the prosecution of the war. He represented that up to the present time no serious attempt had been made to interest Indians in the National Loans; yet he believed that in India there was great wealth which might be successfully tapped for this purpose, and he anticipated great political advantages from the union in financial interests of India and the Empire.

There followed detailed elaboration from both sides on how this might best be brought about, with Chamberlain recommending the Aga Khan fall into line with the general war loan schemes being employed throughout the Empire, and the Aga Khan insisting upon a separate scheme for India on rather nebulous grounds.

A subsequent handwritten letter[10] from Chamberlain to the Chancellor of the Exchequer puts the Aga Khan's offer (perhaps rather ungenerously) in political context:

My dear Chancellor of the Exchequer, I send you a memorandum of a conversation I held yesterday with the Aga Khan [...]. I do not need to comment to you on the difficulties of his proposal, but when the subject arises again I may have to ask you for a Treasury memorandum on the subject to be communicated to him. Personally I feel that there is too much disposition on the part of Indians to overlook the needs of India and the opportunity for helping government there and to think they get more credit and kudos by making their contributions in England. Yours very truly, Austen Chamberlain.

There is more than a hint of scepticism in this communication about the Aga Khan's motives for making a proposal regarding India's role in the financing of the British war effort. It is impossible to prove unequivocally the Aga Khan's motives in doing so. From his general personal and political behaviour described in this narrative, it would seem a case of patriotism, politics and self-interest happily coinciding. The files are silent on the matter from then on.

Turkey's entry into the war

Upon Turkey's joining the war on the side of Germany, concern on the Allied side was significant. London was well aware of the efforts which had taken place for a good twenty years to try to influence the Muslim population of the British Empire into a state of rebellion, and of the subterfuge and intelligence operations conducted by the Germans to achieve this aim.[11] It was also well understood that Turkey, although decaying and split asunder by internal dissent for decades, represented enormous reserves of military manpower and commanded a strategic position, controlling as it did the Bosphorus and thereby naval access to the Black Sea, the Mediterranean lifeline to allied Russia.[12] Now it was realised that no more could be done to keep Turkey out of the war; the ill-conceived and disastrously executed Gallipoli campaign of 1915 was to be the military answer to the new Germano-Turkish alliance.

On the diplomatic front, however, the Aga Khan rushed into action to try to maintain Muslim loyalty to the Allied cause. *The Times* published his 'Message to the Indian Muslims on Turkish Entry into the War',[13] a message which appears clearly calculated to appeal to as broad a Muslim following as possible:

With deep sorrow I find that the Turkish Government has joined hands with Germany, and acting under German orders is madly attempting to wage a most unprovoked war against such mighty sovereigns as the King-Emperor and the Tsar of Russia. This is not the true and free will of the Sultan, but of German officers and other non-Moslems who have forced him to do their bidding. Germany and Austria have been no disinterested friends of Islam, and while one took Bosnia the other has long been plotting to become the Suzerain of Asia Minor and of Mesopotamia, including Kerbela, Nejef and Baghdad. If Germany succeeds, which Heaven forbid, [...] the Kaiser's Resident will be the real ruler of Turkey, and will control the Holy Cities. No Islamic interest was threatened in this war, and our religion was not in peril. [...] Thousands of Moslems are fighting for their Sovereigns already, and all men must see that Turkey has not gone to war for the cause of Islam or for defence of her independence. Thus our only duty as Moslems now is to remain loyal, faithful, and obedient to our temporal and secular allegiance.

There is no way of measuring with any degree of reliability the effect this message had on Muslim public opinion throughout India and indeed the world, but that it was not an entirely spontaneous message from a leading individual becomes clear when reviewing the Colonial Office archives regarding this message,[14] which contain the draft of the text as submitted by the Aga Khan, and the official correspondence surrounding its publication. A note dated 2 November 1914, bearing the India Office seal, reads: 'My dear Read, herewith two copies of the Aga Khan's message to Moslem's generally. H.H. suggests that it sd. be published both throughout the Mahomedan colonies & in East Africa. As regards India, the Viceroy has telegraphed, strongly favouring publication of the message from the Aga Khan. Yours sincerely, etc.'

The note indicates most strongly that the initiative for the message originated with the Aga Khan (with or without prompting, we cannot be certain) but that the imperial authorities seized upon the opportunity it offered without hesitation. The draft text of the message was then considerably sharpened up by some unknown civil servant whose handwriting appears on the draft. The sentence '... has long been plotting to become the Suzerin [sic, MvG] of Asia Minor and Mesopotamia. If Germany succeeds...' as contained in the draft was edited and made more specific and appealing to a wide audience of Muslims. The handwritten corrections and additions make it read as follows: '...has long been plotting to become the Suzerain of Asia Minor and Mesopotamia, including Kerbela, Nejef and Baghdad. If Germany succeeds....'

Hence the message gained in appeal to a broad spectrum of Muslims, by deliberately mentioning specific holy cities at the behest of the Colonial Office. And it was in this form that the text was published. No wonder that the draft text ends with a handwritten comment: 'This message should be published as soon as possible.' The fact that there were a mere four days between the first telegram concerning the message and its final edited publication in *The Times* illustrates how welcome the message must have been to the British Empire at war. In later years, the Aga Khan's lengthy and obviously well-informed (yet anonymously authored) obituary[15] in *The Times* did him no more than justice when it mentioned: '...the Aga Khan took the risk of incurring personal unpopularity by his efforts to soothe the fears of Indian Muslims, and to induce in them a due sense of proportion. His doctrine of the value to both sides of friendship between Great Britain and the Islamic world was of crucial importance.'

Post-war Turkey and the post-war world

The obituary[16] of Aga Khan III in *The Times* mentioned: 'The opportunity for Turkey to make its great recovery after the First World War owed much to his mediation.' Indeed, the Aga Khan played a noted public role in this debate, which however, falls outside the scope of this narrative. However, a Foreign Office file[17] regarding the post-war peace conference contains an impassioned letter[18] from the Aga Khan to the then Secretary of State for India, Edwin Montagu, which was to be described by a British official as his *cri-de-coeur*, and is considered by the author of this narrative to be the most far-reaching statement ever made by the Aga Khan, which resounds to us today in the great events shaping our times:

My dear Mr Montagu, It is not without reluctance that I write you this letter (specially as I know you will be already doing all you can for our cause) but a sense of duty and indeed a sense of loyalty towards His Majesty compels me to do so and to warn you and through you His Majesty's Government before it is too late not to take a step that will have permanently evil consequences not only for India but for the peace of the world. You are free to make any use you like of this letter. Perhaps the Prime Minister and the Members of this Government and [our] generation including myself will not live to see the evils that will as sure as anything follow but that is no excuse. Bismark [sic, MvG] did not live to see the evils of Alsace Lorraine. To turn the Turk out of Europe might have been (with all its terrible consequences to Islam) accepted by a warm and sincere Imperialist like myself if there were one single and real advantage for the B. Empire but alas there is not one that can be advanced that will compare to its disadvantages. To undoubtedly once for all alienate the Moslems of India and Afghanistan and Baluchistan and the Caucasus and the Turkist race merely because purely intellectual reasons having little relation to the facts of life show that to be a symmetrical course is so unlike all the actions and history of England that I still at the last moment pray and hope that Justice for Islam will prevail. No greater mistake could be made than to imagine that the Sultan would in live Stamboul as the Pope does in the Vatican. If his authority as the Civil Ruler of the city is taken he cannot as Kaliph and he will not live in that town he will go to Brusa and all Islam will give him you may be sure its sympathy and approval. Besides Adrianople Threce Constatinople and Asia Minor a line drawn from the North of Mosel and Rawanduz in the East down to the Mediterranean to the north of Alexandretta and including Smyrn[a] and then going along the Black Sea to the old Russian frontier of 1878 that is the minimum that can be acceptable to Islam.

Here, again it is evident that the Aga Khan at the time did not hesitate to speak for Islam as a whole, or indeed did not hesitate to judge what would be acceptable to Islam. Muslim concern about the fate of the Ottoman Empire was also expressed by the Khilafat movement in India, and there is no evidence that other movements in Islam endorsed the Aga Khan's position as a representative for the whole of Islam; but presumably he based this appeal in part on his position as a recognised statesman. The letter continues:

You must make no mistake in India the Indrais Moslem and Hindoo ask for much more besides but here we can rely that if we leave the Turks this their legitimate right we will have in them our best allies to make the Moslems of Asia realise that the Arab separation is in the interest of all concerned. [...] Whatever else happens history never repeats its details. [...] One more fact. If the Sultan keeps Constantinople not only he but all the Turks are always at your mercy and no possibility of his ever joining our enemies for sea power will dominate his capital and air power his coasts. Send him [...] to the highlands of Asia Minor and your are ever face to face with an infinitely more difficult Afghanistan.

Here it would seem that the Aga Khan effectively advocated to the victorious Allies that they retain the Caliphate in Constantinople, more or less to act as a figurehead for Islam, whilst at the same time advising the Allies to ensure that the incumbent Caliph should at all times remain, in effect, under their military control. The letter continues:

Do not make any mistake. If Turkish rule comes to an end no one in India will blame the French or Italians rightly or wrongly English christianity and bigotry will be held responsible and the doctrine that the Turk must even after 500 years go away because he is a Moslem and Asiatic from the sacred soil of Europe will be never forgotten. [...] If the Bolshevists are not to fizzle out if they are to be the danger that Mr Churchill foresees the only geographical and racial areas that can become to civilisation a real danger are the Moslem lands from this very Brusa to Chinese Turkestan. Give Islam as represented by Turkey just and general treatment [...] and you will have your policy successful from Threce to that very Chinese Turkestan that otherwise will for 20 years keep the world in unrest. One last word. India sent one million soldiers to the War. It was India's help that brought Turkey on her knees. Cannot India successfully beg? In her name sure that she will forget her pride and her rights and forgive me this I beg, implore His Majesty's Government to save Constantinople and Adrianople Smyrna and Thrace for the Sultan—Caliph of Islam. I leave my case in your hands and ready to serve His Majesty. Yours ever, (Sgd.) Aga Khan.

[Note: the spelling, punctuation, grammar and underlining are represented as per the original document.]

It is hard to remain intellectually detached when reviewing this message, full of emotion and consequent errors of spelling and punctuation as it is, when one reflects on the situation which today prevails in those parts of the world described by the Aga Khan. Emotion has no role to play in the scope of this book, and to review it in such light must be left to others. Likewise, formally assessing the wisdom of the Aga Khan's statements, and the potential impact on our own times had his warnings been heeded, will be foregone, however tempting. The question of the Islamic caliphate, which ended in 1924 when the Ottoman caliphate was abolished by Mustafa Kemal's revolutionary Turkish government, has become a rallying point of modern Islamist propaganda.

For the purposes of this narrative, we will confine ourselves to observations regarding his relations with the British Government. It is clear that the Aga Khan did not hesitate to address wide-ranging issues to the Government, running the risk of being either misunderstood or ridiculed because his thoughts were so contrary to the spirit of the times. He seems to have acted from a deep sense of dual loyalty: to Britain, and to Islam. Demonstrating far-sighted statesmanship of the highest kind, speaking for Islam, and begging in the name of India herself, he sought to create a settlement for Turkey which would guarantee a prolonged and lasting peace for a region of the world that has been beset by strife. A subsequent memorandum[19] from Montagu to his colleagues in Paris, who were directly involved in creating the peace settlement, commends the Aga Khan's views for consideration, and mentions:

I circulate to my colleagues in Paris the following letter I have received from His Highness the Aga Khan. It is a moving cri-de-coeur and serves to show how a loyal and very moderated Mohammedan, far more moderate than the orthodox, feels on this matter. After all, Indians have a right to a predominant voice in this question, not only because it affects the peace and security of their country, but because they played a predominant part in the conquest of Turkey. Their million soldiers achieved under British leadership the opportunity of discussing this question. I am a little tired of reading in the newspapers the views of Americans (to-day I notice a message from an American Bishop). When I remember that the Americans never fought with Turkey and have now washed their hands of the Peace with Turkey, their right to consideration seems remote. All our Allies are to a greater or less[er] degree in the same position. (Sgd.) E.S. Montagu.

It must, alas, remain one of the great what-ifs of history to ask what might have happened if the Aga Khan's advice had been heeded at this crucial juncture. The events of our time suggest that their impact would conceivably have been considerable, and considerably for the good. The files are silent on his advice from then on. History took its unhappy course.

The rewards of friendship

In an internal note of the Foreign and Political department of the British Government of India,[20] dated 5 January 1920, concerning a complaint of some local prince regarding his status *vis-à-vis* the Aga Khan, the official answer contained the following phrase:

In 1916 the Government of India considered the question of rewarding the Aga Khan for his services in the war. In view of the fact that His Highness's great and widespread influence had been consistently and energetically employed in the service of the Empire, it was decided to recommend him for a salute of 11 guns for his lifetime, together with the rank and status of a 1st Class Ruli[ng] Chief in the Bombay Presidency.

A handwritten addition to the typed text, to be read in at the point of the asterisk in the text, added '...and of the unique [struck out & corrected by hand, MvG] commanding position which he occupies over a large number of Muhammadans.' This official correction confirmed Aga Khan III's unofficial, yet very real, position as a leading figure and opinion-maker among Muslims, at least in British eyes.

Conclusions

From the material examined in chapter 4, it can be concluded that in the prelude to the First World War, Aga Khan III gradually positioned himself as a unifying voice in Muslim public opinion, and presented himself as such to the British. In doing so, he communicated a moderate message and drew the attention of the Indian Muslims, and indeed the wider Indian and Imperial public, to the many benefits brought by the Empire.

Upon the outbreak of war, he became a pro-active and vocal supporter of the British Empire, aiming to unite Muslims worldwide behind the war effort. In doing so, he did not hesitate to speak for the Indian Muslims, or indeed for the Muslim community as a whole, although there is no evidence of him—the representative of only a minor faction of that total Muslim population—being mandated to do so by representatives of the other major movements in Islam.

In the aftermath of war, the Aga Khan proposed a very different peace settlement for Turkey from the one that was eventually adopted, in an attempt to ensure peace for Asia Minor and the Middle East. In doing so, he demonstrated significant emotion, spoke for Islam and did not hesitate to implore in the name of British India. He sketched the dire consequences of the proposed peace settlement (which was eventually adopted) and proposed a radically different way of engaging with Islam, and the territories hitherto ruled by the Turks, by appointing a Caliph who should be firmly under the control of Britain and her allies.

Although this suggestion was ignored, the British Imperial authorities regarded Aga Khan III as a leading figure, an unofficial leader of and opinion maker among the Muslim community; they looked favourably upon his moderate and essentially loyal doctrine.

5

INTERBELLUM

FROM STAUNCH ALLY TO 'A BROKEN REED'
(1920–1939)

Calmer waters

The period between 1920 and 1939 seems to have been one where the relationship between His Majesty's Government and the Ismaili community as led by Aga Khan III was on a largely stable footing. In addition to modernizing his community, the Aga Khan busied himself in particular with the political future of India within the British Empire, and became a leading delegate to the high-profile Indian Round Table Conference (1925–1931), where this future was being debated. His role in this debate gave rise to a very large number of speeches and publications, including such diverse topics as 'The Future of Bombay',[1] 'A Constitution for India',[2] 'The Indian Economic Prospects',[3] and 'Indian Muslim Aspirations'.[4] In these messages we find the by now established doctrine of the Aga Khan: modernist, supportive of Empire, mildly critical at times, yet outwardly always a loyal servant of the Crown. And again we find little hesitation about speaking for the Muslim community as a whole, in this case for the Muslims of India. In 1934, he was sworn in as a member of the Privy Council, that august body of British monarchical government with direct access to, and hence a personal link with, the monarch.[5]

His role in the Indian Round Table Conference is well known but falls outside the scope of this narrative. His interaction with the British Government surrounding his titles and dynastic position at this time will be left to chapter 7. Instead, we will examine a range of interactions with British officialdom on smaller matters which, although they concern less high profile issues, shed a very interesting light on his position as seen by the authorities in London in the two decades between the two World Wars.

Ismaili schools in East Africa

On 23 December 1932, a letter[6] marked 'personal and confidential' was dispatched by an official in Downing Street to Sir Stewart Symes, Governor of Tanganyika. The letter contained the following text:

Dear Symes, I have recently had a conversation with the Aga Khan about the Ismailia schools in Tanganyika which were the subject of your private and personal telegram of 8th October. It appears that he and his community have strong objections to associating their children with Hindus on the ground that they became infected by Hindu influences which they hold in abhorrence. I pointed out to him that the Khoja community were not dissatisfied with the combined schools in Uganda, that we had received no protests from Tanganyika, and the obvious economy of a few large schools over numerous small ones, but he insisted that many protests had been made [...]. Finally the Aga Khan said that if the Tanganyika Government persisted in their attitude there would probably be riots and that in any case the three or four thousand pounds found annually by his community would be stopped. I imagine [corrected by hand, MvG] it may well be that this account is exaggerated, but we are anxious to satisfy the Aga Khan, as he is a valuable asset to us in Indian affairs and has a great deal of influence.

This somewhat charged and passionate exchange with one of His Majesty's most senior civil servants, threatening financial sanctions and indeed even disorder, constitutes quite a contrast with the Aga Khan's public messages of religious harmony and intercommunal peace which are to be found on a regular basis in his public writings and speeches.[7] The British official reaction is equally revealing, describing the Aga Khan as 'a valuable asset to us in Indian affairs'. The Aga Khan was not prepared to let the matter rest after this single conversation with British officialdom. On 21 December 1932 he followed up with a largely typed letter, sent on writing paper with a 'Ritz Hotel, London' letterhead to Sir Philip Cunliffe-Lister, then the Colonial Secretary,[8] containing the following text: 'My dear Sir Philip, [...] after our conversation on Friday last I am enclosing, for your consideration, an aide-memoire about the schools of my people in East Africa. All best wishes, Yours sincerely, Aga Khan.'

Sir Philip was a member of the Privy Council; in addressing the typed letter to Sir Philip, the Aga Khan added in his own handwriting three key words to the otherwise typed address, which read in full: 'The Right Hon. Sir Philip Cunliffe-Lister GBE PC.' A small addition perhaps, but one that was (and is) seen as significant in Britain's corridors of power. Was this a thinly-veiled expression of interest on the part of the Aga Khan in a position as privy councillor, or a sincere correction? The fact that no such corrections are seen on any other letter in the Aga Khan's correspondence reviewed for this book, and the fact that he became a privy councillor in 1934, would indicate the former.

The above mentioned *aide-mémoire* regarding the Ismaili schools, which the Aga Khan attached to the letter to Sir Philip, contains some interesting material regarding the amalgamation of Ismaili schools with Hindu schools, this time using a very different set of arguments against amalgamation:

If amalgamation takes place, in view of the fact that the majority of the Managing Bodies and the staff is Hindu—and they naturally tend towards the National movement in India—the young children at those schools will be unduly influenced in that direction. I here quote Rule No. 167 of our Laws: "It is the tradition with the Shia Imami Ismaili followers of His Highness the Aga Khan to be loyal to and sincerely wish well of the Government under which they may be living, as also to offer thanksgiving to the Almighty on behalf of the Government and obey its laws, to rejoice in its rejoicings and sympathise in its sorrows."

In short, the Aga Khan made it clear that he could vouch for the loyalty of his followers if educational privileges were granted by the British colonial authorities in Tanganyika. The issue dragged on for a number of years, as evidenced by a letter to the Secretary of State for the Colonies from the Deputy Governor of Uganda, C.L. Scott,[9] dated 2 February 1934, which contains the following typed text referring to the matter:

It seems unfortunate that sectional splits in the Indian community should be causing this unnecessary duplication, and in the opinion of your Committee the strongest representation should be made with a view to improving the present position. [...] I understand that the reasons for which many children of the Ismailia community have been withdrawn from the Government school by their parents, are not traceable to any complaint on the part of the latter as to the efficiency of the school. [...] The main cause of these withdrawals is, however, to be found in an agitation fostered by the fear that if children who belong to the Ismailia community attend the Government school the grant from H.H. the Aga Khan, upon which the Community school subsists, will be withdrawn.

If nothing else, this is a clear indication of the degree of centralised control which could be exercised by the Aga Khan over his community throughout the Empire. But also of the extent to which he was prepared to apply pressure to British colonial officials to achieve his goals, and indeed of the circumspect way in which these officials dealt with his requests, however unreasonable and sectarian they may have found them to be. The file which contained the above mentioned letter[10] also contains a typed background document on the issue, with some interesting handwritten comments by unknown officials which shed further light on the importance of the issue: 'In 1930, the Gvt. of Uganda got the agreement locally with the Ismailia Council to close down its school at Kampala.' This clearly indicates that the Aga Khan was not in agreement with the decision of his local Ismaili Council, but chose to overrule them indirectly, via the Colonial Office in London, for unknown reasons. A further handwritten note comments somewhat disdainfully:

Sitting down on a wasps' nest is a nice pleasant pastime compared with tinkering at Moslem or quasi-Moslem sects and their education. If the Ismailia lot want to maintain their own school they will do so and even if the Aga Khan were willing I doubt whether he could tell his followers to go to the Govt. school and say he would give his grant in scholarships. In 1932 he was told that if they wanted to revert to the status quo ante they could do so. We didn't expect that they would just re-open the school and, apparently, not consult Govt., but they seem to have done so.

These are words of an exasperated civil servant, his peace disturbed by the forceful action of the Aga Khan's followers, and apparently questioning their credentials as a Muslim movement.

Further handwritten notes on the same file include some very interesting observations of the behaviour of the Aga Khan as perceived by the unidentified civil servants who wrote them: 'I wish people wouldn't describe the gulf between Hindus and a Moslem sect as a 'sectional split'. To this an unidentified colleague added, also in longhand: 'I agree. H.H. is hot too flush [sic] at present. The question will perhaps solve itself before long. I doubt whether the Aga Khan feared Hindu influences—in fact that seems ridiculous—so much as normal Mohamedon influence.'

Later, in 1934, the issue continued to absorb the time of both the Governor of Uganda and the Colonial Office. On 13 March 1934 a letter[11] was drafted by Sir Cecil Bottomley at the Colonial Office for Sir Bernard Bourdillon, Governor of Uganda, which contained the following text:

My dear Bourdillon, [...] we are frankly disturbed at the idea of coming between the Ismailis in Uganda and their spiritual lord and master, particularly as it seems possible that the Aga Khan had some part (perhaps even a large part) in the re-opening of the school. [...] You will appreciate that, in all the circumstances, the question of an approach to H.H. is not free from delicacy.

Revealingly, the box on the draft letter form with the header 'further action' remains empty. And on 14 March 1934, a letter[12] was drafted by Lord Plymouth, on behalf of the Secretary of State for the Colonies, to the Governor of Tanganyika regarding the Governor's suggestion that the Aga Khan should be approached with a request 'that the grant now paid to the Community School should be devoted to the provision of scholarships at the Government School to be held by children of the Ismailia community.' In his response, the Secretary of State expressed doubt 'whether any useful purpose would be served by approaching him.' The files are silent on the issue from then onward.

Against Bolshevik infiltration—'rather a broken reed'

Completely failing in its endeavours to trigger a Bolshevik revolution in Western Europe, the Soviet leadership of the 1920s and 1930s turned its attention to Asia. 'Let us turn our faces towards Asia, the East will help us conquer the West', Lenin was widely quoted to have said. Hopkirk's book *Setting the East Ablaze*[13] paints 'an extraordinary tale of intrigue and treachery, barbarism and civil war, whose violent repercussions continue to be felt in Central Asia today.' It is beyond the scope of this narrative to revisit these events in detail, but it is fair to say that this conflict was played out in large measure between Britain and Bolshevik Russia, 'for Britain, then still the foremost imperial power, was seen by Lenin as the principal obstacle to his dream of world revolution. "England", he declared in 1920, "is our greatest enemy. It is in India that we must strike them hardest",' according to Hopkirk. It was to prove an intense yet shadowy conflict and, from a British perspective, nothing less than the survival of the Empire in the East was at stake. And in this conflict, the Aga Khan was asked to play a role on Britain's behalf. He was asked to counteract Russian attempts at infiltration in Northern India, acting on information from the British intelligence services.

In a letter[14] marked 'very secret', and sent by the Foreign and Political Department at Simla, the summer capital of British Indian colonial administration, to the India Office in Whitehall, dated 20 July 1933, we read the following:

Proposal to direct the influence of His Highness the Agha Khan to counteract Soviet propaganda. [...] My dear Walton, I am desired to state, for the information of His Majesty's Secretary of State for India, that the North West Frontier Province Government recently received information [...] which has since been confirmed [...] that the Soviet authorities are using three Maulai Pirs, resident in Afghan Wakhan, for the collection of news regarding Gilgit and Chitral affairs. [...] It occurred to Mr Cunningham (as Governor) in the course of consideration of this case that Government should be able to use the spiritual influence of the Ismaili sect in those regions to turn the tables on the Soviet. [...] Any traveller in Chitral and Gilgit cannot but be struck by the immense spiritual influence of the Aga Khan and his agents in those areas and Mr Cunningham therefore suggested the possibility of using this influence to counteract Soviet propaganda, obtain intelligence and spread counterpropaganda. [...] Maconachie was therefore asked on his views on (a) the advisability of approaching His Highness the Agha Khan to bring his influence to bear on his co-religionists who are Afghan subjects. [...] I am now to request that, if there be no objection, the position may be explained secretly to His Highness the Agha Khan who may be asked to use his influence on his followers in Gilgit and Chitral against Soviet agents and propaganda. I am to add that the Government of India propose in connection with this counter-propaganda to use the services of Captain A.S. Shah, Intelligence Bureau, Baluchistan, who is a nephew of His Highness the Agha Khan. Yours sincerely,... etc.

Attached to this note, we find a copy of a memorandum[15] which sets out in detail the observations regarding the three Maulai Pirs:

The following information has been received concerning the three men. 1. Muhammad Akram Khan alias Shah Jahan of Tang lives in Sast about 5 miles below Tang. He is reported to be very cunning and in the pay of Bolsheviks for secret service. He is a tall man, wheaten complexion with medium sized nose. A full beard with a third gone white and aged about 50 years. 2. Arbeb Taghai of Khandut. Is a native of Panja and not Khandut. He is a follower of Pir Abdul Rahman who died last winter. [...] 3. Rajab Beg of Sarhad Wakhan was tax gatherer in the time of Habibullah Khan. [...] He is a follower of Shah Abdul Mohani of Zebak. He is reported to be a very clever man of medium height and middle aged. He has a Jewish nose with a full beard cut short and black in colour. He went to Yarkand last winter and is expected to return this summer. All three men are Maulais by religion. Etc. etc.

Two years later, the issue is still very much on the official agenda, as evidenced by a letter[16] from Lt-Col. J.W. Thomson Glover, His Britannic

Majesty's Consul General at Kashgar (in Chinese Turkestan, described by Hopkirk as 'the northern listening post of the British Empire'), and addressed to the Foreign Secretary to the Government of India, dated 28 March 1935:

> The individual who [...] was moving about with his face covered and was leading the followers of Turdi Mulla had a narrow escape from capture during the Id. While feasting he was surprised by the troops at Damsfar [...] and escaped with some 25 men. Some 150 persons were captured but only 12 of them possessed rifles, some of the others had sticks. Of those captured some 20 are said to have been quietly put to death [...]. In the last two months some 14 men and 4 women have arrived at the U.S.S.R. Consulate apart from the new Consul General and Secretary.

Shortly afterwards, a typed set of minutes[17] of the Political Department of the Government of India, dated approximately 22 June 1935, mentions the approach which was made to the Aga Khan to enlist his support in this struggle, an incentive for him to take action, and indeed the uniquely useful position which the Ismaili movement occupied in British foreign policy:

> Colonel Thomson Glover encloses in his weekly report of 28th March a memorandum on the situation in Sarikol, where the Aga Khan has great influence over the population. Soviet control appears to have made considerable strides in that area and, since Colonel Glovers's report was written, the Soviet have been successful in securing the removal of Mahommed Sharif, the representative of the Chinese Provincial Government in Sarikol, whom they regarded as hostile to them. He has been sent off under restraint to Urumchi. It is of course easy for Soviet propaganda to infiltrate from Sarikol to Hunza and Nagar. [...] In November 1933, Sir Samuel Hoare asked the Aga Khan to use his influence on his followers in Gilgit and Chitral against Soviet agents and propaganda. This His Highness undertook to do. As our request was confined to Indian territory this action was not in conflict with our treaty obligations to the Soviet Union. [...]

At the time, Britain and Russia were attempting to regulate cross-border interactions with a range of treaties which defined their particular spheres of influence in Asia. One is tempted to interpret this as a mutual attempt to impose some rules upon The Great Game. The minutes continue:

> It is suggested that it might be desirable not to remind the Aga Khan of his conversation with Sir Samuel Hoare and tell him that, in view of the increase of Soviet influence in Sarikol, the danger of the Gilgit Agency being affected by communist propaganda is now greater than in the past. [...] No doubt the result of any steps which the Aga Khan can take in the Gilgit Agency to guard

against this danger would penetrate to the Sarikolis. [...] As a matter of fact, if the action suggested in paragraph 3 were taken in conversation with His Highness, the question of the situation in Sarikol would automatically come up, and our purposes would no doubt be achieved by merely drawing his attention to it and leaving him to take what action he wishes in the matter. His own interests would appear to be affected by recent tendencies in Sarikol. Complete Soviet control there would presumably result in a diminution, or even a cessation, of contributions by the inhabitants to His Highness, as, even if communism did not wean the inhabitants from their spiritual allegiance, currency restrictions would, no doubt, make the export of contributions impossible. Thus, it is in His Highness's own interests to combat Soviet influence, and whatever action he takes would have the incidental result of assisting H.M.G. [...]

One can but marvel at the manner in which the Aga Khan was given a personal incentive to take action in the matter, and the subtlety with which he was reminded of the benefits he would personally enjoy of acting in accordance with British wishes in the matter. The text continues:

It is of course necessary to be particularly careful at this moment to keep our treaty obligations regarding propaganda, as we are pressing the Soviet Union on that subject ourselves. On the other hand, although the Aga Khan is a British subject, the Ismailia Sect is not an exclusively British institution and His Highness has presumably a right, of which the Treaty obligations of H.M.G. do not deprive him, to defend the interests of his sect [...] by such means as are at his disposal.

Thus, we have here a clear case of the British Government attempting, by means of the Ismaili movement, to conduct cross-border activities without exposing itself to any diplomatic or political consequences in doing so. In fact, in this particular case the Government was aiming to achieve complete deniability of its involvement in taking steps to counteract Soviet activities.

At the same time, His Majesty's Government was not averse to keeping a close eye on the actions of the Aga Khan in the matter, as evidenced by a subsequent letter,[18] marked *'very secret'*, from the Foreign and Political department in Simla to the India Office in London:

My dear Walton, [...] When the Aga Khan was in Delhi last February Metcalfe took the opportunity of enquiring from him in the course of a conversation whether he had been able to arrange to exert his influence in the manner suggested by Sir Samuel Hoare when he saw the Aga Khan in November 1933. Metcalfe gathered that His Highness had done nothing to speak of in the matter except to send warning to the 3 Pirs named in this correspondence and to certain other of his followers to abstain from intrigues with the Soviet. This impression has been confirmed very recently through a trustworthy but delicate source.

Tantalisingly, one is left wondering who the 'trustworthy but delicate source' is who reports to the British Indian Government on the Aga Khan's activities. The official archives do not reveal who this might have been, but it would seem to have been someone in his close proximity, from the importance attached to the information provided. The text continues:

His Highness' activities in Chitral and Gilgit of late appear to have been devoted entirely to the collection of his dues, and it appears that he has done nothing in the direction of exerting his influence in the manner desired. [...] the Secretary of State may be interested to hear that from all accounts the Aga Khan is proving a broken reed in this matter.[...] He was informed that the Government of India had information, rather vague but very continuous, of some of his followers being suborned, and also of Soviet intrigues. [...] His Highness' reply was that he would make enquiries on his return to Bombay, and would inform Metcalfe of the result. As far as we are aware, this he has not yet done. He also expressed the opinion that the entry of the Soviet Government into the League of Nations would make them more careful than previously about interfering in other countries. In response to a query about his followers in Sinkiang he said that they were all anxious about the present situation as they disliked the chaos and misrule which prevailed under the Chinese. What they expected and indeed hoped for was that the Japanese might succeed in establishing themselves in that Province coming in through Mongolia.

One notes, with the benefit of hindsight, the extraordinary naïvety on the part of the Aga Khan, expecting improved behaviour on the part of the Soviets upon entering the League of Nations, and the painful optimism about Japanese rule in Sinkiang. Perhaps he was a little over-optimistic regarding the role of the League, which may have some connection with the fact that he was to be elected its President a mere two years later.

A short typed note, found attached to the above letter[19] and written by unknown civil servants, states: 'The Aga Khan is, I fear, rather a broken reed in this matter, and it does not seem that any good purpose would be served by approaching him again in regard to it.' A civil servant identified only as 'L' concurred with the handwritten words: 'I agree, L. 29.8'. Thereby the Aga Khan's involvement appears to have ended. There is no further reference to him in the file regarding the matter.

However, a final intelligence report,[20] dated 27 August 1935, is contained in the India Office file regarding this issue, obviously from an unidentified author:

(1) According to information received from Sarikol the Russian Agents in Zarikol have started propaganda in illaqa Sarikol to the effect that the annual subscriptions raised in illaqa Sarikol for Sir Agha Khan should be stopped. (2) Many people in Sarikol say that they had not received any benefit from Sir Agha Khan and therefore the money collected and sent to Bombay should be stopped for ever. Noor Ali Beg, Saugand Beg and Daud Beg, Tajiks, and the residents of Sarikol, who are Russian agents and have been appointed for propaganda work in illaqa Sarikol, carry on vigorous propaganda in this connection. [...] (5) There are two parties of people in (Tajik and Wakhi) in Sarikol. One is pro-Sir Agha Khan and the other is pro-Bolsheviks, and it appears the latter will achieve success [...].

Beyond this, the archives are silent in the matter.

A visit to East Africa

On 9 November 1936, a letter arrived at the Colonial Office regarding a proposed visit of the Aga Khan to East Africa, where a large number of his followers lived at the time. The letter[21] provides a fascinating insight in the nature of the observation kept on the Aga Khan's behaviour by the Colonial Office, and the manner in which discreet assistance was given to make his travels a success:

Dear Wade, His Highness the Aga Khan tells me that he is visiting East Africa early in 1937 and that the Begum [i.e. his wife, MvG] is accompanying him. She, as you probably know is a French lady. His intention is to arrive in Zanzibar in January and after a week there go on to Tanganyika, spending a few days at Dar-es-Salaam and later going by motor to Nairobi. He hopes to do as much sightseeing as possible in Kenya, including another safari. Finally they will leave by air in March. I suppose the position of the Aga Khan is sufficiently elevated for him to command acceptance in East Africa, where social difficulties might otherwise occur and where, perhaps, some comment might be directed from the mixed marriage point of view. It is certainly to be hoped that he will receive all courtesy and consideration, as he is very prominent in the Councils of the Empire and at Geneva. Personally he is a charming and cultured gentleman with a cosmopolitan range of cultural and social knowledge. His wife most worthily upholds her position. Lady Willingdon said to me "she never puts a foot wrong". If you foresee any difficulties, I hope you will give me timely warning, but I hope there is no risk of this and that the Aga Khan carries enough guns to get through. Yours sincerely, J.L. Maffey.

Clearly, on this occasion, the British government was very happy to provide some discreet smoothing of the path for the Aga Khan's visit, without asking for a direct service in return. His standing in their eyes was obviously undiminished at this time, notwithstanding his earlier behaviour surrounding the Soviet intrigues in Asia. The file mentions no controversy regarding the visit.

A clash with the Sultan of Muscat

In 1939, just months before the outbreak of the Second World War, a somewhat confused interaction took place between the Aga Khan and the British government regarding friction between the Sultan of Muscat and Ismailis resident in his territory. The extensive file[22] sheds interesting light on the relations between the Aga Khan and Whitehall at the time, and the (sometimes rather nebulous) services he felt at liberty to request in a semi-official manner. In a letter[23] dated 7 April 1939, and sent on the headed notepaper of Villa Jane Andrée, Cap Antibes, the Aga Khan writes to A.C.B. Symon at the India Office:

Dear Mr Symon, The present Sultan of Muscat is, unfortunately, very prejudiced against my followers out there. I know, too, that he was disappointed that I did not see him and entertain for him during his recent visit to London. At that time I was not in England [...] so I was not able to see him as I wished. I know you were attached to the Sultan while he was in England, and I shall be most grateful if you will write to him and use your influence so that the relations between the Sultan and my people in Muscat may be more friendly in future, and I hope you can persuade him to look on them with a friendly eye. With many thanks, Yours sincerely, Aga Khan.

In response to this, Mr Symon appears to have made inquiries as to the nature of the grievance. This, however, proved somewhat difficult, as a typed internal Colonial Office memo[24] from Mr Symon to a Mr Walton, dated 14 April of the same year, mentions:

Mr Walton, I should be grateful if you would advise me as to the reply which I should make the Aga Khan. The papers in the attached volume [...] show that there was trouble between the Khojas and the Baluchis at Gwadur (there was also a minor incident at Muscat proper) between the years 1929—1932. It will be noted that the Aga Khan approached the Government of India direct in regard to these disturbances, and that the differences between the two communities were settled satisfactorily with the active cooperation of the present Sultan. The Aga Khan's letter to me suggests that the present trouble is between the Sultan and the Khoja community, but even so I assume the proper thing is for him to take up the matter with the local political authorities through the Government of India. My difficulty is to frame a refusal to the Aga Khan without causing him any offence. As you are aware, I have known him for some time and am on quite friendly terms with him.

To which Mr Walton added the following handwritten response[25] in returning the memo: 'Mr Symon, I shd [sic] tell the Aga that you fear you cannot write yourself to the Sultan about a matter of this sort which could only be dealt with officially. Would it not be best for the Aga to explain the case fully to the Gvt who could then consider whether there was any point on which enquiries or representations could be made through our officers in the Gulf. The Aga will remember that the Sultans attitude was quite helpful in the Gwadur case in 1933.' Mr Symon subsequently wrote as follows to the Aga Khan on 18 April 1939, on non-official stationery and without mentioning his formal position:[26]

Dear Aga Khan, I am sorry to lean from Your Highness's letter of the 7th April that all is not well between the Sultan of Muscat and your followers in Muscat territory. We do not appear to have any information here bearing on the matter, and I fear that it is not one which I could raise with the Sultan in personal correspondence. Your Highness may remember that in connection with the incidents which took place in Gwadur in 1930/32 (about which you were in direct correspondence with the Government of India), Sultan Said's attitude was quite helpful, and I wonder whether it might not be best on the present occasion for you to explain the case fully to the Government of India who could then consider whether there are any points on which enquiries or representations could be made through our officers in the Persian Gulf. Yours sincerely (Sd), A.C.B. Symon.

This letter is obviously a gentle testing of the water by a middle-ranking civil servant, who carefully avoids making specific promises and writes in a semi-official capacity. However, the Aga Khan would by no means let the matter rest there. On 25 April, a further letter[27] was received from him by A.C.B. Symon at the India Office, in which he carefully presses his agenda:

Dear Mr Symon, thank you for your letter. I have already written to the Government of India—to Sir A. Metcalfe. I do not want you to write in any way officially, but I thought you might bring about a sort of message of good-will, as you have been so much with the Sultan, explaining that it was only absence from England that prevented me from paying the Sultan a visit and entertaining him during his visit to London because I know he has misunderstood my apparent lack of courtesy. Your sincerely, Aga Khan.

The unfortunate Symon was given no choice in the matter, the issue would not go away quietly. He wrote a short letter[28] to the Aga Khan, after which the matter escalated to higher levels in the India Office:

Dear Aga Khan, I write to thank Your Highness for your letter [...]. I quite understand the position and will gladly explain to Sultan Said that it was only absence from England which prevented Your Highness from seeing and entertaining him during his visit to London. I will do this in my next letter to him. With kindest regards to Your Highness and the Begum Aga Khan, Yours sincerely, (Sgd) A.C.B. Symon.

In this letter the issue of support in a wider sense for the Aga Khan's position *vis-à-vis* the Sultan of Muscat is carefully avoided, and the promised action by A.C.B. Symon is restricted to social niceties. Meanwhile, the correspondence went up the chain of command, both in the India Office and in the Government of India. A typed letter[29] dated 21 April 1939, marked 'Private and Personal', to Sir H.A.F. Metcalfe of the External Affairs Department of the Government of India, from R.T. Peel at the India Office, puts the issue in a wider context:

My dear Metcalfe, I enclose for your information copy of recent correspondence between the Aga Khan and Symon of this Office from which you will see that the Aga Khan is concerned once more about the position of his followers in Muscat State. [...] Between 1930 and 1933 there was trouble at Gwadur between the Khoja and Baluchi communities but the Sultan then took action with salutory results [...] and we have heard nothing from the Gulf of any recrudescence of trouble. The Aga Khan's letter however suggests that it is the attitude of the Sultan himself that is now unfriendly to his followers. We have advised the Aga Khan that his best course would be to have the matter taken up on an official basis through the Government of India [...]. I am not sending copies of this letter or of its enclosures to the Gulf.

Clearly, at this stage of developments, the hope among senior British officials was to induce the Aga Khan to specify his grievances by directing him to official channels, endeavouring to cause no offence, and at the same time not to be drawn into action by his rather nebulous semi-official earlier correspondence. The response letter from Simla arrived shortly. A letter[30] marked 'Private and Personal' from Sir Aubrey Metcalfe to R.T. Peel, dated 2 May, gives another perspective on the reasons for the deterioration of relations between the Ismailis of Muscat and the Sultan:

My dear Peel, [...]The Aga Khan addressed me himself on the 7th of April telling me that he was writing to Symon and stating the position of his followers in Muscat. He was not very precise in his complaints and merely asked me to be kind enough to use my influence with the Sultan, so that he should "look on the Aga Khan's people with a friendly eye." I had correspondence with the Aga Khan on the same subject about a year ago and I then wrote Fowle [...]. Fowle replied in March 1938 that the Aga Khan's followers had nothing really to complain of, but that they had made themselves somewhat unpopular by the truculence of their attitude towards the Muscat authorities. Fowle had seen some of them during a tour to Muscat and had warned them to be more careful. I have now written again privately to Fowle [...]. When I hear from Fowle, I will reply to the Aga Khan and will also let you know what transpires.

Both the India Office and the Government of India were still confused as to what the Aga Khan wanted, and how to proceed. The official correspondence in the matter is marked 'private and personal', a further indication that the Government wished to take no formal position in the matter at that stage. The confusion continued, as evidenced by a letter[31] marked 'personal', and sent on non-official stationery, from The Residency, Bushire on 7 June 1939, to Sir Aubrey Metcalfe, and signed by T.C. Fowle:

My dear Metcalfe, could you please refer to your Personal letter of 28th April [...] on the subject of the treatment of the followers in Muscat of His Highness the Aga Khan, and saying that His Highness had again returned to the charge asking that we should use our influence with the Sultan so that he would look on the Aga Khanis with a friendly eye. His Highness made no specific allegations and no particular requests. You added that you had no idea what His Highness was driving at. [...] I am afraid no more have I! but I imagine that [...] the Aga Khanis are inclined to be somewhat truculent in their attitude towards the Muscat authorities and expect us to procure for them a privileged position in the State to which they are not entitled. However, I am sending a copy of this letter to Hickinbotham with the request that he will find out from the Aga Khanis [in Muscat, MvG] what, if any, definite complaints they have of their local treatment, and in any case to help them as much as is possible.

The full title of T.C. Fowle, the signatory of this letter, was 'The Honourable Lieutenant Colonel Sir Trenchard Fowle KCIE OBE, Political Resident in the Persian Gulf'. On his shoulders now rested the delicate task of finding out whether there were any tangible issues that had triggered the Aga Khan's complaints and request for British official assistance. The task of finding out whether or not any real grievance actually existed in Muscat was entrusted to T. Hickinbotham of the British Consulate and Political Agency, Muscat, who wasted no time in making direct enquiries of the Ismailis in the area. On 19 June 1939 he reported in writing to Sir Trenchard Fowle, in a letter[32] marked 'personal': 'I asked Mukhi Khalfan Murad Ali, the President of the Aga Khani Council, to see me on June 17th. This gentleman informed me that there had been some little differences of opinion in the past but that now they had no question of any sort to bring forward and were perfectly content. I suggested that he should so inform His Highness the Aga Khan.'

One can easily imagine the irritation of the British officials as this message worked its way up through the system to Simla and London. It is perhaps fortunate for posterity that British civil servants were (and are) not easily inflamed in writing. They did, however, administer a semi-official slap on the wrist[33] to the Aga Khan through the Government of India, which, whilst superficially polite, left nothing to the imagination in either the content, the condescending tone or the manner of address:

My dear Aga, In continuation of my letter of the 28th of April about your followers in Muscat, I have now heard that Hickinbotham, the Political Agent, Muscat, has seen the representative of your followers there, and been informed by him that, though there had been some little differences of opinion in the past, at present they had no question of any sort to bring forward and were perfectly content. Your followers thus seem to be quite happy, and I hope there will be no further cause for complaint. With all best wishes, I am, Yours very sincerely, H.A.F. Metcalfe.

It may be considered likely that some internal correspondence within the Ismaili movement followed, and that the Aga Khan himself was none too grateful to his representative in Muscat for being so cooperative with Mr Hickinbotham. We have no evidence of this, and the internal affairs of the movement are outside the scope of this narrative. On the British side, no response appears to have been received from the Aga Khan, and the files remain silent on the matter of the Ismailis of Muscat from that point in time.

For the sake of the father...

In the late 1930s, the matter of the Aga Khan's eventual succession was gaining in importance in British official circles. Although it will be dealt with in detail in chapter 7, below, it can be mentioned here that some attention was given to the behaviour of his son in that earlier period—attention that was polite in written phrase, but nonetheless indicated that he was destined for social oblivion as far as the British Government and royal family were concerned. A Colonial Office file[34] from 1939 regarding the 'Social status of Prince Ali Khan (son of H.H. the Aga Khan) and his wife' was interestingly marked 'Closed until 1990', an unusually long period, which indicates that the Colonial Office must have regarded the contents as potentially painful and damaging to both the Ismaili movement and themselves. The correspondence sheds an interesting light on the delicacy with which any issue to do with the Ismailis was treated, on the position of the Ismailis in Kenya at the time, and on the current and future issues regarding the Aga Khan's son and (perceived) designated successor.

On 7 March 1939, a letter[35] marked 'confidential' was despatched from Government House, Nairobi, Kenya to the Secretary of State for the Colonies by the Governor's deputy:

Sir, I have the honour to inform you that a problem regarding the social duties of the Governor recently arose in Nairobi. The son of His Highness the Aga Khan arrived on the 27th February and the son's wife arrived on the 1st March. They styled themselves Prince and Princess Ali Khan. Their attitude was perfectly correct, they signed the Governor's book immediately on arrival and no fault could be found with their demeanour and courtesy when meeting the Governor. [...] If only for the sake of his father one would naturally wish to shew [sic] Prince Ali Khan hospitality, and he himself is a good sporting type and actually rode in two races during the March meeting in Nairobi. Further, the Aga Khan community in Kenya is above the average for the rest of the Indian community especially in their ideas of loyalty and service, and one would not like to do anything that would hurt their feelings if it could be avoided. [...] But his wife is on a somewhat different footing since, as is well known, her first husband, an Englishman, was granted a divorce against her in 1936 owing to her relations with Prince Ali Khan; and for this reason it appeared undesirable to invite her to Government House.

The Governor's deputy goes on to ask particulars of the social status of the Ali Khan and his wife, and describes some unofficial courtesies extended to the Ali Khan such as 'having them both to tea in my box [at the horse races] which, perhaps illogically, I feel to be on a different footing from inviting them to a meal at Government House.' Subsequently, a despatch[36] marked 'confidential' was sent from the India Office to the Colonial Office which contains the following:

To answer the Governor's questions as listed: (a) Ali Khan and his wife are not officially entitled to be called Prince and Princess. At the last Court Ali Khan attended (before his marriage) he was described as "The Ali Khan" [...] They are however generally known as and called Prince and Princess in society. (b) Ali Khan is not entitled to and should not be addressed as His Highness (c) He has no official precedence [...] (d) Neither of them has been received at His

Majesty's Court since their marriage and their names have not been submitted for entry to the Royal Enclosure at Ascot owing to the divorce proceedings. (e) They are legally married. Yours sincerely [...].

The Governor of Kenya was duly informed of this in a letter[37] from the Colonial Office which conveyed the above information literally. Though businesslike in tone, the correspondence shows that the Ali Khan, then perceived to be designated as future heir to Aga Khan III, was destined to be socially ostracised in Britain; and that for the sake of the father and the relations with the Ismailis, the British extended some informal courtesy to Ali Khan, whilst keeping him diplomatically at arm's length.

Conclusions

Although in the early 1930s Aga Khan III was occasionally perceived by British officials as an irritant, this did not affect the relationship in any fundamental way. And although the Aga Khan sought to influence the Colonial Office in order to get his way regarding the education of his followers in Uganda, the latter evidently attached such importance to him and his Ismaili followers that they refrained from drastic action or confrontation, choosing instead to prevaricate in the matter.

The British and British Indian governments sought to engage the Aga Khan to counter Soviet efforts at propaganda and influence-building on the northern frontier of British India, thereby illustrating the value that he and his wider Ismaili movement were deemed to have for British interests. However, to the disappointment of British officialdom the Aga Khan appears to have taken virtually no meaningful action in the matter. Again, this did not lead to a breakdown in relations. The perception appears to have been maintained that the unique geographical spread of the Ismaili sect was deemed advantageous by London in foreign policy initiatives in countries beyond Britain's sovereignty. However in spite of his extensive information-gathering network, the Aga Khan fundamentally misread Russian and Japanese intentions and future behaviour in the mid-1930s. There is no evidence of any subsequent British judgement regarding the Aga Khan's statements in the matter, but although he was seen as a key ally of Britain, the Aga Khan was kept under some form of monitoring by a 'trustworthy but delicate source' in the mid-1930s, who reported to the British authorities.

As evidence of continued good relations, the British government provided some discreet assistance to smooth the Aga Khan's visit to

East Africa in 1937. On his part, the Aga Khan saw fit to raise issues with the British Government surrounding the treatment of his followers in Muscat. In doing so, he initially avoided official channels and operated 'demi-officially' through his own contacts in the British government. British inquiries made through diplomatic channels revealed these complaints to be a non-issue, and they were interpreted by British officialdom as an attempt to use the British authorities 'to procure for his followers [in Muscat] a privileged position to which they are not entitled'. Again using semi-official channels, the Aga Khan received a rebuke for his actions. This too appears not to have detrimentally affected the British-Ismaili relationship, since in 1939 the colonial authorities in Kenya took care to extend informal courtesy to the son of Aga Khan III, while keeping him diplomatically at arm's length.

6

WAR CLOUDS AGAIN
(1939–1953)

General observations

Those files which might contain information on the Aga Khan's (and wider Ismaili) efforts for the Allied cause in the years leading up to the Second World War, and during the war, are comparatively thin. It might be surmised that any records of the more secretive services which a movement that was widely dispersed, both geographically and ethnically, such as the Ismailis might have rendered are subject to prolonged closure under the Official Secrets Act. However, from the material currently available, it would seem that at least part of the explanation for this apparent lack of activity must be found in the advanced age and continued ill-health which plagued the Aga Khan at the time. In his later obituary[1] in *The Times*, some mention is made of this period of the life of the Aga Khan, and hence of the Ismaili movement:

When the Second World War broke out, he was on the Riviera, and on the downfall of France he went to Switzerland for medical treatment, remaining there throughout the war period. Apart from the immediate issue of a manifesto to his followers enjoining loyal support of Britain, he was unable to play any notable share in promoting Allied aims as he had done in the 1914–1918 War. He was not seen in England until the summer of 1947. There were critics who felt that he should have managed somehow to leave France for some part of the Empire he had so long served. He had, however, a succession of illnesses [...].

From this it appears that the role of the Aga Khan in the war, and indeed the activities of his followers, was significantly less wide-ranging

61

than in the First World War. The Aga Khan issued, as he seems to have done three decades earlier, an edict to his followers to encourage them to remain loyal to Britain. Neither the first nor second of these manifestos could be recovered from the files by the author. They must therefore be assumed to have been internal to the Ismaili movement, if they were indeed issued, as no copies have been preserved in any of the official British archives consulted.

However, the issuing of such a statement to all Ismailis reminding them of their duty to remain loyal to Britain, while attractive from the British point of view, would have contravened one of the key laws of the Ismaili movement which, as we saw in the previous chapter, the Aga Khan himself saw fit to explain to Sir Philip Cunliffe-Lister in 1932: 'I here quote Rule No. 167 of our Laws: "It is the tradition with the Shia Imami Ismaili followers of His Highness the Aga Khan to be loyal to and sincerely wish well of the Government under which they may be living, as also to offer thanksgiving to the Almighty on behalf of the Government and obey its laws, to rejoice in its rejoicings and sympathise in its sorrows".' One must presume that this would also hold for the Ismailis in, say, Vichy France and Vichy-dominated Syria and North Africa, or indeed in Chinese Turkestan. How this dilemma was resolved, or whether it was perceived as a dilemma by the Ismailis, remains unclear. Perhaps such concerns were overridden by the need for *taqiyya*, as was so often the case in earlier centuries of Ismaili history.

The absence of major initiatives on the part of the Ismailis and the Aga Khan does not imply that there were no contacts with the British government at all in this period of their history. Indeed, in the lead-up to the war and during the aftermath, there were some notable exchanges that shed an interesting light on the perceptions of His Majesty's Government regarding the Aga Khan and his Ismaili movement at this time.

Horse Trading with the British Government

Shortly after the outbreak of the Second World War, there occurred an episode in Ismaili-British relations that was embarrassing to both the Aga Khan and (a decade later) to the British Government. On 24 October 1939, a letter[2] was despatched by the Aga Khan to the Secretary of State for India, the Marquess of Zetland, which contained a rather embarrassing admission:

My dear Secretary of State, I am very sorry to inform you that I am in serious financial trouble. Before going any further I must explain to you how it all happened. I invested between £500,000 and £1,000,000 in horse flesh. [race horses] [...] It was a wonderful concern, the best gilt-edged investment possible until Mr Hitler upset my apple cart—like those of so many others. Now my position is one of great and serous difficulty. When I made investments [...] I had to contract debts with banks. I now owe roughly £275,000 to Coutts and Lloyds Bank.

The fact that the above letter is written on paper headed 'Hotel Ritz, Place Vendôme, Paris' puts the Aga Khan's difficulties at this stage in some perspective. It continues: 'In these circumstances my position is now very serious. I wish to make an offer, through you, to His Majesty's Government placing the full facts before the departments concerned, to sell all the animals on the enclosed lists to the Government for £ 129,000. Personally I think it is the best business proposition they will have during the War.'

In his own mind, the Aga Khan must have felt he was indeed supporting His Majesty's Government, in his own unique way. The letter continues: 'In this connection I may explain that the stud farm to which I refer in Ireland belongs to my son Aly, whom you know well. I can arrange with him that for the duration of the War he should rent to His Majesty's Government the stud farm, its lands and buildings, at a nominal price provided rates and taxes are also taken over.' Indeed His Majesty's civil servants knew Aly only too well, as we saw in the preceding chapter, and will see again in the following chapter dealing with the succession to the Imamate. Meanwhile, the horse-trading went on as follows:

The price I have quoted you is for His Majesty's Government only. At this price I would not in any circumstances sell to private buyers [...] It is my very natural desire that what has cost me an enormous sum of capital, as well as immense work and labour, should go to the nation rather than to others who will make a fortune out of it. I must tell you very frankly that I am already in communication with buyers in America and Italy, to whom I have quoted very different—and very much higher-prices. [...] I would only earnestly request that my offer does not become known to breeders who, once they knew that I had quoted such excellent terms to His Majesty's Government, would try to squeeze me.

Here, the Aga Khan, despite his English education, uses language which may have been considered somewhat unbecoming by the recipient. The tone of this exchange is out of character by comparison with

all his previous correspondence, since it appears more suited to bar-
gaining in a commercial environment than becoming of a respected
elderly statesman who is referring a sensitive personal issue to His
Majesty's Secretary of State for India. It is probably best to see in it an
illustration of His Highness' despair at the time.

Just to make sure the point about the attractiveness of the offer was
not missed, the Aga Khan added a postscript to the letter: 'P.S. Please
ask the Government departments concerned not to mention my price
to anyone outside as it would seriously prejudice me.' There followed
a lengthy description of his stallions and mares, their names such as
'Fille de Salut', 'Friar's daughter' and 'Turtle soup', and their respective racing and breeding achievements. British officialdom considered
the offer very carefully indeed, as may be surmised from draft letters[3]
to Sir Eric Machtig and Sir Allan Barlow, both senior civil servants,
which examine the wider political considerations of the offer: 'As you
will realise, any consideration of this offer must be affected by the
nature of our existing and future relation with Eire [...].' At the time,
relations between Britain and the Irish Free State or Eire were on an
unsure footing, as the bloody confrontations between the British Army
and the Irish independence movement (not to mention the violent
internal dissent among Irish Republicans) had left deep scars and
resulted in much mutual recrimination at the political level.

The note continues:

I enclose herewith a copy of a letter from the Aga Khan [...]. The Aga Khan's
offer of his breeding stud to the Government at a figure well below the market
price appears on the face of it an attractive financial proposition, but it also
raises some difficult and knotty questions of policy with which several Departments are concerned. [...] The Dominions office also come into the picture,
since any consideration of the proposal must take into account our present and
prospective relations with Eire, while the Aga Khan's special position in the
Moslem world may give rise to special political considerations [...].

Interestingly, upon examination, the file does not show any decision
being taken by the government departments concerned. Presumably, in
the bustle of a war which was for the first three years a very close-run
thing indeed, His Majesty's Government lost sight of the issue. It
would, however, resurface many years later, in a most unexpected
way. In the obituary[4] of the Aga Khan which appeared in *The Times*
in 1957 we read: 'The Aga Khan's relative immobility due to illness led
him to respond to many suggestions that he should write an autobiog-

raphy. This was dictated at his villa above Cannes and published in 1954. [...] The Aga Khan derived from his father a love of horse flesh. [...] It was unfortunate that he saw fit to export his successful sires, thus losing that valuable result of endeavour and clever thinking to British bloodstock breeding.'

Two decades after the original correspondence, the statements made by the Aga Khan regarding his proposal to sell his bloodstock to the British Government would lead to some official agitation at the Ministry of Agriculture, as shown by an internal memo[5] dated 11 February 1955, apparently responding to a suggestion by a Mr Burrell that the statements made by the Aga Khan in his autobiography concerning this matter should be refuted in the magazine *Sporting Life*:

I entirely disagree with Mr Burrell's suggestion that a correction of this kind should be made through the columns of the "Sporting Life". This would immediately have the effect that Mr Burrell seeks to avoid, namely involving the Minister personally with the Aga Khan. In view of the Aga Khan's position, it would not only be discourteous but most impolitic to take the matter up in any other way than direct with the writer, if it were taken up at all. [...] Mr Burrell's own recollection is at fault. It is not the fact that the Aga Khan's offer (made at the end of October, 1939) was accepted. The offer was still under consideration when it was withdrawn on or about 10th December. [...] Of course, I appreciate Mr Burrell's feeling that his judgment has been criticised by implication. [...] I think this is one of the things that a Civil Servant is bound to suffer in silence.

It is clear, then, that either the Aga Khan's patience or his financial resources ran out while His Majesty's civil servants prevaricated, and he sold off his bloodstock to foreign shores. It is equally clear that in the early stages of the Second World War his stature in British official circles, and the importance attached to Ismaili goodwill, was such that any message from him was treated with some care. The files are silent on this issue from then on.

A claim against the French Government

As mentioned above, in the Second World War the ageing Aga Khan appears not to have been perceived as active in his support for Britain and her Empire in the way he had been in the Great War. But with extensive properties and possessions in occupied territory, most notably France, the pro-British Aga Khan suffered losses which he sought to recuperate after the war.

A Foreign Office file[6] contains extensive correspondence about the Aga Khan's lost Rolls-Royce car, which occupied British officials in the immediate aftermath of the war. A note[7] from the British Embassy in Paris to the Foreign Office also mentions the Begum Aga Khan's car, and seeks to have the car released from the French military authorities which had (presumably) recovered it from German requisitioning, or had taken it after the liberation of the South of France. Indeed, the file preserves a note[8] from the British consul in Nice, which states, 'Several cars have been requisitioned in my district by French military and civil authorities stop My protest of no avail so far stop Should I insist or are requisitions in order.' The telegraphic reply[9] from the British Ambassador in Paris was not long in coming: 'You should continue protests. If still ineffective refer specific cases to me.'

This British official interest in the Begum Aga Khan's car seems to have triggered similar interest from the Aga Khan himself. A telegram[10] was received which mentions, rather tersely: 'My representative monsieur Plisson trente quatre quai Henri quatre Paris has found my Rolls Royce which was stolen by Germans in 1940 I will be most grateful if you will kindly help with authorities for its been return [sic, MvG] to my ownership [...]'.

British officialdom sped into action. Later that month, a letter[11] was sent to the Aga Khan by the British Consul General in charge of the War Damages Department: 'Sir, [...] I have the honour to report that instructions have been given by the Ministere des Finances for the release of this car, now at Oloron, and that same will be handed to your Highness' representative through the British Consulate in Bordeaux.' In the comparatively minor matter of recovering confiscated cars, and immediately following the conclusion of the war, the British authorities were clearly happy to be of assistance in the recovery of these vehicles. However, some years later, the Aga Khan returned with bigger claims, and this time the response was to be different.

On 3 May 1953, a letter[12] was received at the British Embassy in Paris from the Ministère des Affaires Etrangères, direction des Affaires Economiques et Financières, which mentioned:

Invoquant les dispositions de l'Accord de réciprocité franco-brittannique [...] l'Aga Khan et le Prince Aly Khan ont saisi le Ministère de la Reconstruction d'une demande d'indemnité de dommages de guerre relative à la perte de chevaux de course. [...] il est indispensable de déterminer au préalable si les intéressés remplissent les conditions exigées par la loi du 28 octobre 1946 sur les dommages de guerre et notamment s'ils étaient sujets britanniques à la date du sinistre.

This triggered a letter[13] from the consular section of the British Embassy in Paris to the Foreign Office in London, enquiring as to the nationality of the Aga Khan and Aly Khan. The response[14] must have been a shock to the Aga Khan when it was eventually conveyed to him:

The Aga Khan and Prince Aly Khan are at the present time British subjects without citizenship and potential citizens of Pakistan. There are not, and were not at any time, so closely connected with the United Kingdom or with one of the Crown Colonies that we could deem them to be British subjects "from" the United Kingdom [...]. We are advised therefore, that the Anglo-French War Damage Agreement [...] is not properly applicable to the cases of His Highness the Aga Khan and Prince Aly Khan. [...]

The files do not mention whether any other action was taken, or whether some other arrangement was made to reimburse the Aga Khan and Aly Khan for their losses. It must remain a matter for speculation whether the British official response would have been different if the Aga Khan had played a more openly active role on the British side during the Second World War.

A visit to King Farouk of Egypt

During the turbulent years following the Second World War, the Aga Khan paid a visit to King Farouk of Egypt, and the records show that he reported his observations to the Foreign Office, which took a keen interest in Egyptian affairs. A letter[15] to Sir Ralph Stevenson, the British Ambassador in Cairo, from a Mr Bowker at the Foreign Office, dated 18 May 1951, illustrates the importance attached to the information thus obtained: 'My dear Ralph, Thank you so much for your most interesting letter [...] sending an account you had from the Aga Khan of his talk with King Farouk and his new Queen. Your letter was sent to read by the Secretary of State. [...].' [Note: the corrections were made by hand in the original document, MvG]

The letter[16] to which he referred gives an interesting insight into British diplomatic intelligence-gathering and the role played therein by the Aga Khan, as well as a none-too-flattering account of the then King and Queen of Egypt:

His Highness the Aga Khan and the Begum have been here since Sunday morning, the 6th May. They flew here at the pressing invitation of King Farouk who sent a personal telegram to the Aga. [...] They dined with us à quatre on Tuesday and on Wednesday evening they had a private dinner with King Farouk and Queen Narriman. [...] I arranged to see the Aga on Thursday in case the King and he had had any political conversation of interest. The Aga told me that King Farouk was apparently much enamoured of his new Queen. [...] He expatiated on the steps which he had taken to prepare her for the sharing of his Throne and continually fished for compliments on the finished product. The young Queen (she is only 17) struck the Aga Khan as being a very self assured young person and one with ideas of her own which she was not shy to ventilate. [...]

The marriage between King Farouk and his Queen Nariman Sadeq was not to last long. When the King was exiled after a coup d'état in July 1952, she initially joined him in exile but returned shortly thereafter to Egypt; they divorced in 1954. The letter continues:

During the dinner the King said practically nothing of political interest except that he made it clear to the Aga Khan that the wedding present which had given him the greatest personal pleasure was that from King Leopold of Belgium who, he said, had also been misunderstood in the past and whose actions and attitude had now been vindicated. Apart from that the King's only interesting statement was incidental to a discussion of the present hot weather in Cairo and was to the effect that it was worse in the Sudan, to which country it was impossible to persuade Egyptian officials to go as they always insisted on resigning rather than being transferred there. In his few contacts with the King during his time here the Aga did however gather that he took a realistic view of the world situation and was most anxious to avoid any kind of a break with Britain.

Thus the Aga Khan did not hesitate to pass on sensitive information to Britain regarding a Head of State whom he befriended, information he had acquired during a convivial private dinner; nor did British officialdom hesitate to approach him for such sensitive information regarding a friendly Head of State. It is highly likely that the British Government had some doubts about King Farouk's judgement and hold on power at the time, and the Aga Khan's visit must have proved a convenient means of assessing the King's behaviour.

The same despatch furthermore contained a statement from the Aga Khan which must be considered, more than forty years later, just as politically relevant today as when it was originally made:

The Aga Khan also told me that he had recently visited Teheran and Damascus and the thing which struck him as being of the most vital importance was the necessity of Britain and America speaking with the same voice in the Moslem world. Nothing would produce a worse effect than if it were thought that we and the Americans differed over Middle Eastern policy. "The Americans must back you up" he said.

It is outside the scope of this narrative to rule on the correctness of this statement by the Aga Khan concerning the unity of purpose of Britain and the US on Middle Eastern policy. This will be left to other researchers, and indeed to commentators. However, it is once again direct proof both of the statesmanship of Aga Khan III, and of his wish to make his information and indeed his views available to the British government.

Conclusions

Aga Khan III, and hence the wider Ismaili movement, appear to have been less active for the British cause in the Second World War than in the Great War of 1914–18. In spite of this, the various British government departments dealing with the Aga Khan's offer to sell his entire bloodstock of horses to the Government still treated his messages with some care because of his position and perceived wide influence. As a small but positive gesture, support was given in the recovery of the Aga Khan's car after the war, but no support appears to have been forthcoming in supporting his post-war claim for damages against the French government. In the correspondence regarding this matter, his formal British nationality was considered non-existent for the purposes of the war damages treaty between France and Britain.

The Aga Khan provided sensitive information concerning King Farouk to Britain, which he obtained in personal conversation with that King while meeting under conditions of friendship. For their part, British officials did not hesitate in approaching him for this information, clearly indicating the value to Britain of the relation with the Aga Khan and his movement. As a further indication of this value, the Aga Khan offered advice to the British Government on the alignment of British and American policy in the Middle East, following visits to Damascus and Teheran.

7

THE QUESTION OF THE SUCCESSION
TO THE IMAMATE
(1953–1958)

General observations

Of the many official British government files recovered or consulted for the purposes of this narrative, none were more voluminous than those files dealing with the succession to Aga Khan III. The intensity of correspondence, and the seniority of those involved in the making of key policy decisions (some of which would involve taking action in the name of the Queen), illustrate the great importance attached to harmonious relations between the Ismaili Muslims and Britain. The files of the Colonial Office, and those of the constitutional department of the Dominions Office, were marked 'Secret' and 'Confidential' respectively. Much of the correspondence contained in the related Foreign Office file was likewise marked. The material contained in these files sheds light, more than any other material previously examined, on the intimate relations between the Ismailis and Britain at this crucial juncture of their interlinked developments. Britain, coming to terms with the end of Empire and the cruel blow of the failed intervention in Suez, was seeking a new role for itself in the post-war, and indeed post-Empire, world order. The Ismailis, scattered around the world and as often as not located in geopolitical unstable areas or racial trouble spots, more than ever required the steadfast support of an old friend. As we shall see, in this new world order the British government kept a proprietorial eye on the delicate issue of the succession to the Ismaili Imamate. It was an issue which would redefine and reaffirm the relationship between the British government and the Ismaili Muslims. This also shows, with remarkable clarity, the unwritten contract which cemented this continued relationship, and which (presumably) holds till the present day.

There was, as will be seen, a significant difference between the formal and public role of the British Government in this regard and the actual influence exerted behind the scenes. In a copy of a note[1] dated 15 June 1955, responding to a question by Major C.E. Mott-Radclyffe, MP, the official position of Her Majesty's government on the succession to the Ismaili Imamate is set out by Douglas Dodds-Parker, a Conservative politician highly regarded as a specialist in the field of foreign policy and quiet diplomacy, with a superb war record, who was then Parliamentary Under-Secretary of State at the Commonwealth Relations Office. He writes: 'You asked me about the recognition of a certain successor. As I thought, this is not in any case a matter for H.M.G. We would, I imagine, treat as the rightful successor, whoever was chosen by his followers as the new leader. There is, however, no question of our recognition being required. (Sgd.) Douglas Dodds-Parker.' To which note we find a handwritten addition, stating 'Can we have a word sometime?' Details of the resulting conversation are not recorded in the official files.

Thus, the Government formally stated to a Member of Parliament, and thereby put on the public record, that it would accept any successor chosen by the Ismaili followers. In actual fact, as the files show, there was never any question of this choice being made by the followers of Ismailism. Instead, it would be made by the Aga Khan, in close consultation with the Her Majesty's Government, who had some unique leverage to influence the matter, as we shall see.

Preparations for a Death

Some two and a half years before Aga Khan III passed away, senior British civil servants commenced correspondence concerning the reaction of the Government to such an eventuality, and to the official response that would be required from Buckingham Palace. In a typed draft letter[2] dated 13 February 1955, from Mr Antrobus at the Foreign Office to K.W. Blaxter at the Colonial Office, we read:

It has been agreed between our two Departments [...] that the Colonial Office would be primarily responsible for advising on the affairs of the Aga Khan. In view of recent reports on the state of his health—though he made some remarkable recoveries in the past—it seems that one might expect to learn at any moment that he had a fatal seizure. Questions relating to the succession may, therefore, assume some degree of urgency at almost any time [...]

To this the following handwritten text was added: 'We assume that if the Aga Khan should die the Colonial Office would assume responsibility for any messages of condolence from H.M. the Queen and from the U.K. Govt. You would no doubt keep in touch with us on this.'

Thus, the responsibility for the official handling of the foreseen passing away of the Aga Khan was allocated in the civil service, and we may conclude that the question of succession was one in which the Foreign Office and the Colonial Office would take a keen interest.

A wayward son

As we saw in a previous chapter dealing with the relations between the British Government and the Aga Khan in the lead-up to and the early days of the Second World War, some doubts had already been expressed by senior civil servants in official correspondence[3] as to the standing and character of the Aga Khan's then perceived successor, his son the Aly Khan. This concern again found expression in British official circles as the matter of the eventual succession began to gain in importance in the mid-1950s. In a typed note[4] marked 'personal' from Sir G. Laithwate to Douglas Dodds-Parker, we read: 'Mr Mott Radclyffe, M.P., has had a fly dropped over him about the "succession" by the Aly Khan: will H.M.G. "recognise" him as Aga when the present Aga Khan dies, in view of his wild-oat-sowing?'

It was this question which gave rise to the official answer which was reported in the first paragraph of this chapter. The note, however, gives some tantalizing, if diplomatically phrased, unofficial detail. In the first place it mentions that the previously identified Member of Parliament had 'a fly dropped over him', an analogy from the fly-fishing sport, and a clear indication that he was stimulated, indeed provoked into asking this particular question at the behest of some other person. Alas, it cannot be ascertained from the official files who this person might have been. In the second place, in typical British fashion, the note expresses a clear judgement of the perceptions of the Aly Khan's lifestyle. Describing someone's behaviour as 'wild-oat-sowing' in official circles was a coded yet damning reference to high-life and womanizing. In short, not the sort of public behaviour which Her Majesty's Government could condone in a spiritual and temporal leader upon whose loyalty and service the government would perhaps have to rely in future. With this simple note, it is abundantly clear what position the British government would take in the matter. As we shall see in a succeeding paragraph of this chapter, the Aga Khan himself understood only too well the vulnerability caused by this situation.

The title of the successor—'once the attitude of the Khojas is known'

In the official British correspondence concerning the preparations for the eventual death of Aga Khan III and the succession to the Ismaili Imamate, much attention is given to the continuance of the title 'Highness'. In a draft note[5] between the Colonial Office and the Foreign Office, dated 13 February 1955, we read:

We thought it might be useful to look into the question of His Highness' titles. This we did and the results were embodied in a departmental note of which I enclose a copy. It is quite clear from the records that the grant of the title "Highness" derived from the Aga Khan's position as the spiritual head of a Muslim sect community in India and that he had not any territorial stake in the country which would have entitled his son to succeed him as a ruling Prince. It The Title was, in effect, of purely ceremonial significance and was granted to the Aga Khan on a personal basis. It is equally clear that, even if India had remained in the pre-August 1947 position in relation to the Crown, the question whether the Aly Khan (as the Aga Khan's heir) would have been granted the title "Highness" would have depended on whether he succeeded to his father's position as the spiritual head of the Khoja community, i.e. as the leader of the Ismaili sect in India.

[Corrections reproduced from the original document.]

The paper[6] attached to this document also sheds some interesting light on the matter. Presumably written by one or more unidentified civil servants, and dated 16 February 1955, it puts the title and position of the Aga Khan in context. It recalls:

In April 1916, the Aga Khan [III, MvG] was granted a salute of 11 guns and rank and status for life of a First Class Ruling Chief of the Bombay Presidency, distinctions which had not been accorded to his father or grandfather. A claim by the Aga Khan in 1925 that the status accorded to him was intended also to carry with it such fiscal privileges as a First Class Chief of the Bombay

Presidency would enjoy in the matter of exemption from Income Tax and Sea Customs, was rejected on the grounds that such qualified exemptions from British Income Tax as the Inland Revenue allowed to Indian Rulers was based on personal immunity from jurisdiction of Court arising out of their "sovereignty" whereas the status accorded to the Aga Khan in 1916 did not carry with it a recognition of sovereignty and he remained a British subject. In 1938 the Aga Khan addressed a Memorial to the Viceroy begging that the honours conferred upon him as personal distinction [...] should be made permanent and that his status should, at the same time, be regularised by the grant to him of the immunities and privileges admissible to ruling Princes, including exemption from Income Tax assessment and from customs duties on goods imported for his personal use.

The effect of acceding to his request would, of course, have been to enable his son, Aly Khan, to inherit the honours and privileges of the Aga Khan on the latter's death, which would in turn have removed the substantial leverage which London could exert over the Aga Khan. The note continues:

The reply, which was sent to him with the concurrence of the Secretary of State for India, confirmed the 1925 decision that he was not entitled to the fiscal privileges and reminded the Aga Khan that the notification conferring upon him the rank and status of a Ruling Chief of the First Class in Bombay was intended merely to regularise his position vis a vis Ruling Princes within the domain of ceremonial honours and courtesies. He was also reminded that the title of "Highness" and the pension which accompanied it were first bestowed on his grandfather in recognition of his spiritual leadership of the Ismaili Khojas and for his life time only. After his death it was again granted for his life time only to his son. [...]

The above shows that British officialdom was not always able to distinguish between Khojas (originally Hindus who converted to Ismailism) and the Ismaili community as a whole. The note continues:

He was therefore informed that it was not possible to offer a guarantee that similar privileges would be conceded by H.M. the King to His Highness' son until the occasion had arisen and the attitude of the Khojas was known. The letter informing him of this decision—it was dated 8th September, 1939—then continued as follows: "but although, as Your Highness will appreciate, it is impossible in these circumstances to give any definite promise in advance, there is every reason to hope that it will be possible to make a submission to His Majesty the King Emperor recommending the grant of the personal title of "Highness" to your son when he has succeeded to Your Highness' own position as the spiritual head of the Khoja community.

Here we see, gently and carefully phrased, British colonial diplomacy at its most effective. High honours were bestowed, on which a reputation and indeed a worldly position rested, in no small manner. But they were bestowed conditionally, with the hope held out that they might be renewed at some future date 'once the attitude of the Khojas was known'. Repeated attempts to make the title hereditary, or at least hereditary in a *de facto* manner by granting fiscal privileges which would put the title on a similar footing to those that were already hereditary, were ever so politely refused. The note also makes some interesting observations regarding the Aga Khan's position since Indian independence:

The position of the Aga Khan in India since the 15th August 1947 is somewhat obscure. The 'Ruling Princes' concluded accession agreements and merger agreements with the Government of India in accordance with which their territories are now embodied in the Indian Union. The agreements safeguarded the continuance to the former Ruling Princes of such personal privileges as they enjoyed before that date and they retain their titles in India and in the United Kingdom. [...] So far as is known, no agreement of any kind has been concluded by the Aga Khan with either [India or Pakistan, MvG] and his privileges (if he still enjoys them) must rest on the most nebulous of foundation.

Hence, the Aga Khan had good reason to bear the likely views of the British Government in mind in any proposed action surrounding the succession. And as we shall see, he took great care to take these views into account.

A consultation with Sir George Allan

The archives[7] contain a handwritten note from early April 1955 which passed between two senior civil servants of the Colonial Office, stating:

We must be grateful to the C.R.O. for the extremely useful note which they have prepared on the Aga Khan. Now we have assumed responsibility for him, it will be for our S. of S. [Secretary of State, MvG] to arrange suitable message of condolence when the Aga Khan dies. The succession will presumably be in the hands of the Ismailia Communities in the various parts of the world, but there may be other matters which we shall have to think about, such as titles and gun salutes.

They were to be much mistaken in their assumptions on how the succession was to be arranged. A note[8] to a Mr King, dated 14 April 1955, signed by Mr Kisch at the Colonial Office, declared:

Mr King, the letter [...] is a timely reminder that we should have everything ready so far as possible against the death of the Aga Khan which in the nature of things may occur at any time. As regards message of condolence I suggest we will require messages from the Queen to the Begum and "Prince" Aly Khan, the latter also expressing condolences to the Ismaili Community as a whole (this is on the assumption that Aly Khan succeeds to the Imamate). Similar messages will also be required for the Secretary of State to send on his own account. [...] There is one other point. This position of the Aga Khan's successor is a unique and rather personal matter and it might be worth considering whether we should not mention the matter on a confidential basis to the Aga Khan's Legal Advisor, [...] otherwise there might be some danger of confusion and hurt feelings later if the next Aga Khan sees matters in a different light than we do.

Their assumption of the Aly Khan succeeding was to be proven incorrect, but the note illustrates that the Government was keen to prevent confusion and hurt feelings. Clearly, a good relationship with the future Aga Khan was desired. A meeting with Sir George Allan, the Aga Khan's legal adviser, was duly arranged, as a note[9] testifies:

Sir George Allan, the Aga Khan's Legal Advisor, came to the Office on the 23rd June for a discussion on matters relating to the Aga Khan's successor. [...] Sir George Allan was unable to say definitely who the successor was to be though he felt sure that the Aga Khan would have committed his choice to writing among his personal papers. He did, however, say that in his own opinion the Aly Khan was most likely to succeed. [...] and Sir George considered it most improbable that the Aga Khan would, against precedence, oust his eldest son.

In this, Sir George was to be proved mistaken, as wisdom would overrule tradition and precedence. However, he helpfully mentioned that 'it was unlikely that the leaders of the community would dissent from any edict by the Aga Khan whose decisions were venerably respected', thereby illustrating the strong centralised control exercised over the worldwide Ismaili Muslim community by the Aga Khan.

The matter appeared to be settled. However, on 27 July 1955, a note[10] was despatched marked 'Secret, by hand', from Sir George Allan, at his premises in Hanover Square in London, to W.A.C. Mathieson at the Colonial Office:

Dear Mr Mathieson, As I informed you on the telephone a few days ago, I saw His Highness The Aga Khan during his recent visit to London and explained to him the various points which you would like to be clarified. His Highness was kind enough to dictate a note to me himself, two copies of which I enclose. I shall be glad to call and see you after you and your colleagues have had an opportunity of perusing the note.

The following day, this exciting and unexpected development triggered a note[11] from the Colonial Office to the Commonwealth Relations Office, illustrating the importance of the issue at hand: 'Dear Gibson, You will remember the discussion we had on the 23rd June about the Aga Khan and the succession to the Imamate with Sir George Allan. I now enclose a letter he has sent to Mathieson [...] with an interesting enclosure. It appears that Sir George Allan would like to see us on Tuesday next, 2nd August.'

The attachment[12] to these letters sheds most interesting light on the Aga Khan's preparations for his succession, his wishes in this regard, and the requests he makes to Her Majesty's Government in connection with it. In some regards, it forms his temporal and political testament:

SECRET—Note dictated by H.H. Aga Khan to Sir A. George Allan on 19th July, 1955. The problem of Succession to the Imamate has already been solved as far as humanly can be done, but it is in the hands of God in this way what happened to my father and my brother and myself could happen again. A year before his death my father appointed my eldest brother as his successor, but my eldest brother died a few months afterwards and he had no sons but only daughters and I succeeded my father automatically under Moslem Law as his sole male heir (with my mother) and no question ever arose afterwards. Moslem Law is clear and understood, inheritance going by nearness at all stages. In the present case, to the knowledge of all the leading members of our Community both in Africa, Asia and the Near East, and especially in Irak, by an immediate proclamation which has already been prepared, my grandson, the eldest son of my son Aly, will succeed and should he be dead (which God forbid) his brother, Aly's second son, will succeed me.

It is noteworthy that the Aga Khan makes a special mention of his followers in Iraq. Was this triggered by the internal politics of that country at the time? Or was there some internal dissent among the Iraqi Ismailis? The files are silent on the matter, and the Aga Khan did not elaborate. He continues:

The reason given for Aly to retire in favour of his two sons is that, in the interest of the Ismaili Community, it is advisable after a long Imamate of already 70 years, that the Succession should go to a young man, brought up in the New Age of Nuclear Physics, the contraction of the World by aerial navigation and the various important changes in habits and conditions that are taking place. Aly, being already a middle-aged man of 45, his background would still be that of the motor age and not that of the future.

No mention here of wild-oat-sowing by Aly, but the fact that the Aga Khan uses the term 'the reason given for Aly to retire' strongly suggests that this was to be merely the outward manifestation of a decision taken on the grounds of more pressing internal considerations. The note continues:

As the Imam is the sole guide of the Ismaili Community, it is in the interests of the Ismailis that his mentality should be such as to be built to direct their religious and secular further development according to the new conditions of the second half of this century. [...] As the Colonial Office know perfectly well, there are vast properties all over Asia and Africa, from Malaya to the Middle East, Irak, Syria, Egypt, right up to Cape Colony (such as schools, school buildings, Prayer houses, Burial Grounds etc.) that are not private properties in the strict sense but still go by inheritance, and there would be very serious legal complications in the case of my eldest son's death before me and the natural heir, my second son, being passed over, which he would certainly resent and oppose. In view of these facts, although all the Leaders of the Ismailis know perfectly well and men like Sir Vazier Eboo Pirbhai could, in confidence, tell the Government what the arrangements are, especially in the view of the dangerous life that Aly leads riding races, Point-to-Points, fast motors, private aeroplanes, etc. neither myself nor the Leaders of the Community could risk a public appointment. All the proclamations are ready and should I have the good fortune of not having a sudden death [...] the proclamations would be published.

In short, Her Majesty's Government was being asked to act as guarantor of an orderly and dignified succession in case of his death. He continues:

The advice, which I myself, with humility, offer is the following: My Grandfather, when he came to India was on account of his Persian position, addressed by Lord Parmerston [sic] and Lord Dalhousie, then Governor General, as "Your Royal Highness" in all official communication. When he settled down in India, the British Government conferred on him the title "His Highness" as a personal distinction and gave him a big pension. [...] Now the Empire of India has disappeared, so, in fact though not by precedence, my rank of Ruling Prince has disappeared.

The Aga Khan then explains, in some detail, his credentials and services previously rendered to Britain, before coming to the key point:

In case of my death, what I would seriously advise in the interest of Her Majesty's Government, (who will always have in some part of the Empire, a great many Ismailis as well as Ismailis in the Middle East, such as Syria, Irak, Iran, Afghanistan, Chinese Turkestan), the title of "His Highness" should be conferred as a personal distinction but without a pension, on my successor for his life time. Thus, as far as we can reasonably look forward, all the benefits of the present association of the Imam with the British Government will continue and yet no permanent ties will have been established which might be of disadvantage later on in the distant future for the British authorities. In the case of my death, it would be advisable that a personal message of condolence should be sent to my wife from the Person of the Sovereign, while the Government, as such, could condone with my Successor and, in the interests of everybody concerned, give him a strictly limited life title of "His Highness", but, of course, no Ruling Prince or Salute or Pension.

Thus, the Aga Khan offered the deal of a lifetime, through the mediation of Sir George Allan. Britain would enjoy the continued loyalty of the Ismailis worldwide, and indeed 'all the benefits of the present association of the Imam with the British Government'. The Ismailis in turn would benefit from an orderly transition of authority, with Britain acting as guarantor for the arrangement and as the provider of temporal status and recognition. And both parties would enjoy the benefits of a suitable enlightened successor, without making unconditional promises for the future. One can but marvel at the excellence of the arrangements, and the manner in which they were brought about.

Although no written answer was given to the Aga Khan, it is safe to assume that Sir George Allan returned with a verbal message indicating the agreement of Her Majesty's Government. As we shall see, both sides accepted the professed arrangements with alacrity. Honours and telegrams were to be the contract.

The moment of succession—titles and telegrams

On 11 July 1957, a short and somewhat terse telegram[13] was sent from Her Majesty's Consul General in Geneva to the Foreign Office, marked 'En Clair': 'PRIORITY—I much regret to report that His Highness the Aga Khan died at Versoix at 12.30 pm July 11th.'

Such a short message to announce the end of a long and fruitful life. It was the trigger for the Whitehall apparatus to get into action, which would involve action at the very highest level of Her Majesty's Government. In reaction to this news, Alan Lennox-Boyd, one of Britain's most senior politicians of the time, who was then Secretary of State for the Colonies, wrote a memorandum[14] to the Prime Minister:

PRIME MINISTER, As you will have seen, the Aga Khan died yesterday. [...] On my advice the Queen has already sent a message of condolence to the Begum and will be sending a suitable message to the Aga Khan's successor. I have also arranged for messages from Her Majesty's Government. I understand that the Aga Khan's body is to be kept in Switzerland for four or five days and that the funeral is then to take place some day next week at Aswan in Egypt. [...] I feel strongly that H.M.G. should be represented at the funeral in view of the Aga Khan's long record of loyalty and co-operation, though I quite recognise that there might be difficulties in overcoming the formalities which might be imposed by the Egyptian Government. If these difficulties could be overcome, and if you agree, I would like to suggest that the Governor of Tanganyika, Sir Edward Twining, should be asked to represent H.M.G. at the funeral. There is a large Ismaili community in Tanganyika and the Governor was personally well known to His Highness.

Some days later, the information department of the Colonial Office issued a public statement[15] concerning this representation:

His Late Highness the Aga Khan. Governor of Tanganyika to Represent Her Majesty's Government—Her Majesty's Government have nominated Sir Edward Twining, Governor of Tanganyika, to represent them at the funeral of His late Highness, the Aga Khan, which is to take place at Aswan in Egypt later this week. [...] The good offices of the Swiss Government have been invoked to secure Egyptian agreement to Sir Edward Twining's journey to Aswan.

This representation was to give rise to a very detailed and indeed amusing report from Sir Edward Twining which, since it is not immediately relevant here and is rather lengthy, is contained in the Appendices attached to this book. Both in humorous style and in content it rather resembles Evelyn Waugh's classic novel[16] of colonial life entitled *Black Mischief*. It triggered a formal acknowledgement from the soon-to-be-notorious John Profumo, then Parliamentary Undersecretary for the Colonies, which is also contained in the Appendices.

Meanwhile, a telegram[17] had been despatched, of which the drafts have been preserved in the official archives. On 12 July a telegram marked 'En Clair' (i.e not in code) was sent from the Foreign Office to Geneva: 'Please pass the following to the Begum Aga Khan from the Prime Minister. Begins. Please accept my deep sympathy on the death of His Highness The Aga Khan. Harold Macmillan. Ends. (Copies sent to No. 10 Downing Street.)'

There was, according to the archives, a flurry of similar messages from Her Majesty's Government and indeed from Buckingham Palace. And the response was not long in coming. On 23 July the new Aga Khan wrote[18] to Selwyn Lloyd, Secretary of State for Foreign Affairs:

Dear Secretary of State, allow me to thank you for the great honour Her Majesty's Government showed my beloved grandfather and my family in sending His Excellency Sir Edward Twining to accompany my grandfather upon his last journey. On behalf of my family and myself may I express our deepest gratitude to Her Majesty's Government. As the successor to my grandfather, may I assure you that I will do my utmost to maintain the good relations between Her Majesty's Government and the Ismaili community, which was the continued policy of my grandfather. I hope that the community will continue to contribute to the peace and prosperity of the territories under whose laws and protection they live. Yours sincerely, Aga Khan.

To which Selwyn Lloyd answered on 29 July, in a letter[19] addressed to 'Prince Karim Aga Khan' (n. that the title 'Highness' had not yet been bestowed!): 'Thank you very much for your letter of July 23. I was touched by your expression of gratitude and by the assurance that you would work for the maintenance of the good relations between Her Majesty's Government and the Ismaili community. [...] With sincere assurance of good will, (Sgd.) Selwyn Lloyd.'

Meanwhile, in the background in Whitehall, some debate was still ongoing regarding the bestowal of honours, which made it clear that not all of Her Majesty's civil servants were entirely well informed on the relations between Britain and the Ismailis. A (draft) letter[20] from Sir C. Dixon at the Commonwealth Relations Office to W.A.C. Mathieson at the Colonial Office, marked 'confidential' and presumably written in the days after the announcement of the death of Aga Khan III, mentions:

I have spoken to Gibson who attended the meeting on the 23rd June, 1955, to which you refer, and he tells me that, whatever he may have said at the meeting, he was not to be regarded as having agreed to this proposal on behalf of the Commonwealth Relations Office. We are, in fact, somewhat doubtful about its desirability. [He is referring to the bestowal of the title of 'Highness', MvG.] [...]. In any event, it seems to us somewhat doubtful whether in the altered circumstances the conferment of such a title on the head of a religious sect is, from a general point of view, now appropriate.

This draft was marked 'Not to go' by hand, so it is safe to presume that shortly after he wrote his draft, Dixon was informed as to the arrangements made between Her Majesty's Government and Aga Khan III. Nonetheless, Dixon seems to have asked for guidance from his Secretary of State, and thereby must have found out what had been agreed. He quickly changed position, as evidenced by a memorandum[21] sent a few days later on 18 July 1957:

Dear Mathieson, [...] the matter has been submitted to our Secretary of State whose view is as follows. The late Aga Khan was a very good friend of ours and had a long record of cooperation and we may hope that we shall over many years, if all goes well, receive a corresponding degree of support and assistance from the new Aga Khan, who will be, as his Grandfather was, a spiritual and not a temporal potentate. In all the circumstances Lord Home supports the idea that the Personal title of "Highness" might be conferred on the new Aga Khan.

And so it was to be. On 2 August, a telegram[22] went out to the UK High Commissioners in India and Pakistan, marked 'Priority, En Clair', which stated: 'Dignity of "Highness" for Aga Khan. In view of his succession to the Imamate and to his special position as Head of the Ismaili Community, many of whom reside in Her Majesty's Overseas territories, Her Majesty has been graciously pleased to confer upon the Aga Khan the Dignity of "Highness".'

The day before, a letter[23] with attachment[24] had been despatched to Aga Khan IV himself, now addressed as 'His Highness the Aga Khan', from Alan Lennox-Boyd, copies of which were preserved in the official Foreign Office archive:

It gives me great pleasure to send you with this letter a formal notification of The Queen's approval of the Grant of the dignity of "Highness". This news will be released by the Colonial Office, on behalf of the Palace, at noon tomorrow, the 2nd August. [...] I was very touched to see the kind letter which you sent the Foreign Secretary about Sir Edward Twining's presence at your grandfather's funeral as the representative of Her Majesty's Government. (Sgd.) Alan Lennox-Boyd.

The attachment to the message states: 'Your highness. I have it in command to inform you that, in view of your succession to the Imamate and your position as spiritual Head of the Ismaili Community, Her Majesty The Queen has been graciously pleased to confer upon you the dignity of "Highness." (Sgd.) Alan Lennox-Boyd.'

And thus the relationship between the Ismaili Muslims worldwide and Her Majesty's government was formalised for another generation.

The aftermath of succession

Although Aga Khan III had made, as we have seen, extensive arrangements surrounding his succession, there were some loose ends in which the British government played a semi-official role.

On 10 September 1957, a letter[25] was received, addressed to Secretary of State Lennox-Boyd, from the wife of the late Aga Khan, appealing for his help in securing her position and temporal status:

Dear Mr Lennox Boyd, [...] I now take the liberty of seeking your advice on a confidential matter, as I know the affection you have always shown my husband and myself. I would like to know what is my correct position now. I am under the impression that I remain the Begum Aga Khan until the new Aga Khan gets married, but I read in the Press so many different titles ascribed to me [...]. As you know, Matasalamat is the highest religious title of our sect and was given to me by my husband eleven years ago, but of course I never use it except vis a vis the Ismailis. I would like to know if I still have the right to use "Her Highness" as during my husband's lifetime or if there is any change so far as I am concerned. Please forgive me for troubling you about this detail, but I respect your advice as an old and sincere friend, and shall be most grateful for it. Will you please remember me most kindly to your wife [...] At the moment I am happy to have the new Aga Khan with me here and we have a lot to discuss together before he leaves for the long tour of visits to all his followers, as my husband expressed in his will: 'I desire that my successor shall during the first seven years of his Imamate be guided on questions of general Imamate policy by my said wife the Begum Aga Khan who has been familiar for many years with the problems facing my followers and in whose wise judgement I place the greatest confidence.' I thought you would be interested to know this, and it is a great consolation to me to still be able to be of service to our followers in this way. With kindest regards, and every good wish, (Sgd.) Omthabibeh Aga Khan.

A subsequent internal government letter[26] of 18 September 1957, to Mr D.L. Cole, considers the matter, and gives guidance on a response which would not compromise the British government:

Dear David, the widow of the late Aga Khan has recently sought Mr Lennox-Boyd's advice on a number of matters in a personal letter. These include whether she remains the Begum Aga Khan until the new Aga Khan marries and whether she still has the right to use the title "Her Highness". We shall naturally advise Mr Lennox-Boyd to keep clear of saying anything which might conceivably be interpreted as taking sides in a dispute within the Ismaili sect, and it is scarcely for him to say whether or not the late Aga Khan's widow should continue to style herself the Begum Aga Khan. [...] It would, however, presumably be for Mr Lennox-Boyd to give advice on the continued use of the title "Her Highness". I have consulted the Private Secretary at the Palace about this and they say "once a Highness always a Highness." Perhaps, therefore, you would confirm that the C.R.O. have no objection to Mr Lennox-Boyd giving this advice.

And so it was to be. In a letter[27] dated 27 September 1957, addressed to 'H.H. The Begum Aga Khan', Lennox-Boyd answered:

On my return from Italy I have found your letter of the 4th September asking my advice on various points. I am sure you would not expect me to advise you on matters affecting your title, which are the concern of the Ismaili sect rather than Her Majesty's Government. But in so far as the title of "Her Highness" is concerned, I can confirm that it would be customary for you to continue to use it during your lifetime. It is kind of you to think of asking us to a meal. I certainly look forward to seeing you again soon, but as my wife leaves tomorrow on a visit to the States and I myself am off to East Africa for a month on October 4th I fear it would be difficult to arrange anything just at present. (Sgd.) Alan Lennox-Boyd.

And thus the matter was concluded. There is no further reference to the matter in the official files.

The joy of a 'doctor of watches'

The official records show a flurry of messages and acknowledgements, through Foreign and Colonial Office channels, from the Ismaili councils across the globe expressing their joy at the bestowal of the title 'Highness'. Usually these were communicated through Governors and deputy Governors to Whitehall and received an appropriate formal answer. None of these need to be recalled here, since they add little to the purpose of this narrative.

However, the archives preserve one slightly unusual message,[28] sent from Kampala, Uganda and dated 3 August 1957, which went straight to Buckingham Palace. It is here represented in the original:

To, HER IMPERIAL MAJESTY THE QUEEN, BUNKINGHAM PALACE. MAY IT PLEASE YOUR GRACIOUS MAJESTY? My family and myself much pleased to learn that, Your gracious Majesty has so kindly conferred the most high esteemed title of "HIS HIGHNESS" to our new Imam Karim Aga khan, on realising and appreciating the Dignity and his position as spiritual head of the 20000000, Ismailis followers. We heartily thank your gracious Majesty on this occasion and we trust your Majesty will continue your affection and love towards our new Agakhan, as in the past late Kings and Queens have done so to our late Agakhan. Our best wishes to your Majesty and all the members of your Royal family. Anxiously awaiting your most esteemed acknowledgement. Thank you. I am under your most excellent commands. Yours sincerely, Hassanali. J. Hemani. Doctor of Watches.

The response to this correspondence could not be recovered from the archives, but one presumes that under the long-established policy of Buckingham Palace that every letter is answered, some form of acknowledgement was sent. And that for many years, a framed and proudly displayed letter from the Palace must have hung in the shop or home of Mr Hassanali J. Hemani, Doctor of Watches.

Conclusions

From the material examined in chapter 7, it may be concluded that the British government took a keen interest in the matter of succession of the Aga Khan, and played an active role in the succession process. The government did not view the succession of the Aga Khan by his wayward son, the Aly Khan, in a positive light.

The Aga Khan, through his legal adviser, made arrangements for the succession with the British Government. Under these arrangements, the grandson would succeed to the Imamate, with the British government acting as enablers for an orderly transition and as provider of temporal status.

Both the Aga Khan (III) and the British Government frequently referred to mutually interlinked interests, and to the benefits enjoyed by both sides resulting from the close relationship. Subsequently, the newly installed Aga Khan IV made unequivocal statements of cooperation with Britain at the time of his accession to the Imamate, and was bestowed significant public distinction and honour by the British Crown, which further cemented and institutionalised the relationship between Britain and the Ismaili movement.

However, the British government did not bestow public honours automatically and in perpetuity across the generations, and the correspondence examined makes it all too clear that the future bestowal of such distinctions depends on the behaviour of the Aga Khan, his heirs and successors, and the movement as a whole. Thus the relationship between Britain and the Ismailis, although mutually beneficial, was subject to review and continued scrutiny.

8

FIRMLY ESTABLISHED AS A FRIEND OF BRITAIN
(1955–1969)

General observations

As may be seen from previous chapters, Aga Khan III was considered by British officialdom to be a friend of Britain and her Empire, and a very loyal and indeed useful ally. The purpose of this chapter will be to examine a number of interactions between Aga Khan III and Aga Khan IV, on the one hand, and the British Government on the other around the time when the question of succession was discussed. This period of Ismaili history may be seen as a crucial test of the Ismaili-British relationship, since it would determine whether this relationship depended on solely on the person of Aga Khan III, or would continue during the Imamate of Aga Khan IV and thus be on a more stable footing.

A visit to Syria by the Aga Khan's representative

The files[1] of the Levant Department of the Foreign Office for 1955 make reference to a visit to Syria by Mr Hassam Kassim Lakha, the semi-official representative of Aga Khan III, in order to 'organise the Ismaili community there.' Even the front cover of the file gives a clear indication as to the purpose of the visit, and the role played by British diplomats in arranging it: 'In view of the Syrian attitude to minorities, it is not proposed to give Mr Lakha political countenance, but commercial help will be given.' The enclosed correspondence sheds interesting light on the intertwined interests of Britain and the Ismaili Muslims at the time, and on the mutual support rendered.

On 23 March 1955, a letter[2] marked 'confidential' was sent from the British Embassy in Damascus to the Chancery of the Levant Department:

Our Commercial Department recently received a visit from a certain Hassan Kassim Lakha who claimed to be the Aga Khan's representative in Syria. [...] We are not certain of Mr Lakha's nationality, but we think it probable that he is a Pakistani. He claims to be a Director of the Uganda Coffee Curing Company Limited and of the Masaka Cotton Company Limited, both of Kampala, Uganda. [...] He claimed to have been sent by the Aga Khan to organise the Ismailis in Syria; and said that he hoped to raise their standard of living by improving their cotton crop and by finding suitable markets for it. [...] We have no independent source of information about Mr Lakha, but his story is inherently plausible.

No documents were preserved in the archives showing whether a check was performed on Mr Lakha's credentials in the Ismaili movement. If indeed such a check were omitted, that would seem remarkable. The message continues:

There are believed to be about 50,000 Ismailis in Syria. They form fairly close and well-defined communities with their centre at Selemiye. [...] While we do not wish to discourage Mr Lakha's commercial interests which could be valuable to us, we are somewhat chary of him from the political point of view. It is true that the Ismailis are only a small community and, in general, get on well with their orthodox Sunni neighbours, but the Syrians do not like foreigners meddling in their internal affairs or even knowing too much about them, and this is particularly the case with minorities. We do not, therefore, propose to give Mr Lakha any political countenance, if he should ask for it, or to help him in any way except commercially.

This was a clear indication that, using the channels and (indeed the convenient cover) of regular commerce, the British embassy was quite prepared to support the Aga Khan's envoy in his work, albeit while keeping a low diplomatic profile. On 31 March 1955, a letter[3] from the Commercial Secretariat of the British Embassy in Damascus to the Commercial Relations and Exports department of the Board of Trade in London shed further light on Lakha's visit:

...we have recently been visited by a gentleman from Uganda, who says that he has come to Syria on behalf of H.H. the Agha Khan, to assist the Ismaili community here. [...] The purpose of this visit is to organise the 50,000 Isma'ilis here, with a view to improving their standards of living. Cotton growing and exporting is to be encouraged, with particular emphasis on quality. [...] The scheme, which seems to us to be admirable, if it can be worked, is to export on a co-operative basis the cotton produced by the community. [...]

Beyond this, the file makes no mention of Lakha, nor of the success or failure of his mission. It may however be surmised, from the positive tone of the above correspondence, that he did indeed gain the cooperation of the commercial department of the British Embassy in Damascus. The future development of the Ismaili community in Syria falls outside the scope of this book.

It is worth noting that the subtle and slightly underhand approach taken by the British Government in supporting the Syrian Ismailis in 1955 differs greatly from the attempted British intervention in judicial trials of Syrian Ismailis some fifty years earlier, as studied by Douwes and Lewis.[3] These trials, ostensibly on charges of murder, attempted murder and use of violence in collecting money for the Aga Khan, appear to have been inspired by the desire of the Ottoman Empire to prevent the wider Ismaili movement from re-connecting with their long-isolated former fellow-Ismailis in Syria. In this, the accusations of murder and other crimes appear to have been a convenient tool to achieve wider political aims. Although the British Government was initially slow to react, many representations were made by the British Ambassador on behalf of the accused to the Ottoman authorities. Douwes and Lewis report that initially the appeals failed, and may even have damaged the interests of the imprisoned Ismailis. Subsequent efforts by British diplomats to intervene in the matter are shown to have had unimpressive results.

There is no evidence to suggest that the more measured support given by the British to the Ismailis was directly inspired by the lessons learned some fifty years earlier. The changed, and indeed much diminished, position of Britain in the world may have been an equally important factor in choosing a more low-key approach in supporting attempts to bring the Syrian Ismailis once again under the central control of the Aga Khan in the 1950s. What is certain is that Britain remained ready to support the interests of the movement, and was willing to render practical assistance in bringing erstwhile followers back into the fold of the movement, even though it must have been aware that the government of Syria would not have approved of such actions.

Reports on the Followers of the Aga Khan in Pakistan and East Africa

The Foreign Office archives[5] for 1955 contain some brief status reports on the followers of Aga Khan III in Pakistan and East Africa, and a description of their social and political attitude at the time, highlighting the continued interest in the behaviour of the Ismailis in routine reporting. A letter[6] dated 18 May 1955 to the Commonwealth Relations Office says:

Dear Bromley, [...] we can only speak about his followers in Pakistan, where there is a fair sized community of Ismailis. From the information available here they seem to be pretty well integrated with the rest of the Muslim population. They certainly do not dabble in politics as a community. They are principally traders, and give the impression of being relatively better off than most other sects, perhaps because of their extensive welfare and charitable organisation which, I believe, is a feature of the sect wherever it flourishes. [...] At a 'weighing' ceremony in Karachi in Fe. 1954 the Aga Khan [III, HvG] was reported by our High Commissioner to have said in a speech: "You Ismailis know perfectly well that it is a fundamental point in your religion that wherever you be, whatever the State, where life and honour are protected, you must give your entire loyalty and devotion to the welfare and service of that country." His followers in Pakistan seem to live up to that principle.

It is noteworthy that the Aga Khan added the proviso that loyalty to a host state was mandatory 'where life and honour are protected'. This was not evident in similar statements of the mandatory loyalty of Ismailis to a host state which we examined in previous chapters.

In the same archive we find a letter[7] dated 16 July 1955, from the Colonial Office to the Foreign Office, regarding the Ismailis in East Africa, which gives a similarly favourable view:

Dear Bromley, [...] The Aga Khan is the spiritual and temporal leader of his Ismaili community and he has a great deal of influence over them. In East Africa his followers look towards the welfare of Muslims throughout the territories and devote their energies to the improvement of social, educational and economic standards rather than to political aspirations. The Aga Khan has fostered in his subjects loyalty to the authorities in whichever country they choose to settle and his example has induced the community to accept East Africa as their home and identify their interests with those of the country of their adoption. It is an acknowledged fact that his strong leadership has done much to encourage the assimilation of Ismailis with the rest of the population and, so far, nationalist movements originating from outside have met with little support from his followers in East Africa. [...]

It is evident from both items of routine correspondence that Her Majesty's Government took a favourable view of the activities and the socio-political attitude of the Ismailis in Pakistan and East Africa in 1955, when the Ismaili community was in the last years of the Imamate of Aga Khan III.

A Proposal for the Ismaili Community in South Africa to move to East Africa

The British official archives[8] have yielded documents showing that in 1958, shortly after Aga Khan IV assumed the Imamate over the Ismailis, a highly sensitive issue developed over the future of the Ismaili community in South Africa. The Aga Khan sought the help of Her Majesty's Government in the matter, which—given the wide ranging implications—may be considered a serious test of the strength and depth of the relationship between Britain and the new Aga Khan.

On 8 July 1958, a letter[9] was sent to the Earl of Home, Secretary of State for Commonwealth Relations, from Alan Lennox-Boyd, the Colonial Secretary already mentioned, which contains the following:

The Aga Khan came to see me today. Among the points he raised was his anxiety about his Ismaili community in South Africa. There are very few of them—only about 300—and though a few are in Durban, nearly all are in Pretoria. Under the Group Areas Act they have got to move out of their homes in a period between one and seven years and will neither be able to live nor practise business except in the areas allotted to them. [...] The Aga Khan is deeply anxious to find something reassuring he can say to his community. I feel that with such dreadful legislation as in South Africa there is very little we can do, but I would welcome your comments about it. (Sgd.) Alan Lennox-Boyd.

Some days later a letter[10] was received in reply, which betrayed the Earl of Home's personal opinion of the South African legislation:

My dear Alan, [...] You are right, I am afraid, in thinking that there is really nothing that the United Kingdom Government can do, since we have no locus standi. The chances are that all, or nearly all, of the Ismailis are Union nationals through birth in what is now the Union of South Africa. [...] I am, of course, always ready to see the Aga Khan but in these circumstances all I could do would be to take up the non possumus attitude. All this does not as you know mean that I would not like to help defeat current Union legislation, but simply that it is not our business and that we are helpless. (Sgd.) Yours ever, Alec.

However, the Aga Khan would not let the matter rest there, and was working on a solution for which he would require British support, and which sheds an interesting light on the inner workings of the Ismaili movement when faced with such an issue. On 19 August a letter[11] was received by Alan Lennox-Boyd from the Aga Khan:

My dear Alan, when we met I mentioned to you my difficulties in regard to my community in South Africa. The Group Areas Act which has come into force and is now being implemented is very oppressive to the Ismailis, and it seems as if the position will get progressively worse. They, therefore, would like to move en bloc. Although the Government of South Africa will allow them to leave the Union, at present it is adamant about not allowing any of them to take their capital out of the country. I believe that £500 a year is the maximum they can move. Moreover the Union authorities insist on treating them in the same way as all the other Indian, and do not recognise that they have a special position. In fact they do not differentiate between Muslims and Hindus. [...] If it is possible to move my community, I think it would be best first to find a place for them to go, and then make representations to the Union Government. The Ismailis in South Africa comprise some 65 families of approximately a total of 400 persons, men, women and children. They have a certain amount of capital varying from £500 to £10,000 with a total, perhaps, of £350,000 (counting the three or four big businesses.) From these numbers approximately 40 families will want to leave South Africa. [...] The East African Councils suggest that the best place for them to go would be Tanganyika, and I would be very happy indeed if this were possible.

This reference to the Aga Khan's consultation of the Ismaili Councils in East Africa sheds an interesting light on the manner in which he related to the wider Ismaili community when dealing with a crisis or issue; the fact that he bases his arguments on the advice received from his councils indicates that his rule, although undoubted and revered, did not transgress into the autocratic in matters such as these. The letter continues:

The Councils have suggested that it might be possible to find some suitable land in the Western Province near Lake Tanganyika, and some of them could settle on the land and grow crops including coffee, while others could engage in trade, motor transport and, I believe some would be prepared to set up small industries [...] which could help with the economic development in that part of the Territory. Tanganyika is most attractive to the Ismailis of the Union and I know they would adopt the country in every way. Would it be possible for you, Sir, to represent the case to His Excellence the Governor of Tanganyika, and ask him to consider sympathetically the question of these unfortunate people [...] I feel confident that this relatively small increase in the number of Ismailis in the Territory will be of no harm to it, and, I hope, very much to the contrary. [...] In the event of the Union Government not permitting them to remove their money, I would have to see whether I could find sufficient finance to establish them in Tanganyika or such other territory where arrangements could be made for them to stay. I should be most appreciative of any help you can give me in this very difficult problem, and I hope that you will forgive such a long letter. With kindest regards, (Sgd.) Yours ever, K.

In addition to shedding some light on the inner workings of the Ismaili movement, this letter must be considered most revealing in a number of other ways too: the easy confidence with the Aga Khan approaches Her Majesty's Government with a problem he knows to be diplomatically complex, his detailed insight into the finances of his followers in South Africa, and his ability to use the network of the worldwide Ismaili Councils to find a place for resettlement.

Furthermore, he offers no financial charity as such: the Ismailis of South Africa will have to use their capital to resettle unless this proves impossible. Only then will there be financial support. In the meantime, the Aga Khan offers practical diplomatic help. It may be considered that in this regard the Ismailis embraced the current principles of successful overseas development several decades before the large aid organizations of Western Europe started to embrace similar principles in their activities.

The archive[12] contains subsequent correspondence between departments of the British Government following that request from the Aga Khan. In a letter[13] marked 'confidential' and dated 16 October 1958, to the Governor of Tanganyika, Sir Richard Turnbull, it is mentioned that 'The Secretary of State [for the Colonies, MvG] is very much concerned over the fate of these families and is anxious that we should do all we can to help both them and the Aga Khan.' However, there was to be an unexpected response. On 17 November a reply[14] was received from the Office of the Chief Secretary at Dar es Salaam, which mentioned:

My dear G.B., In the absence of the Governor on safari I am replying to your letter [...]. The Governor agreed the lines of this reply before he left Dar es Salaam. There are strong and overriding political reason which make the Aga Khan's proposal not only unattractive but indeed very objectionable. In the first place, we could not ignore the construction which would be put by various parties on a decision to take in these Ismailis. And at the present time the Ismailis are probably the least popular of all the Asians in Tanganyika. Our recent intelligence reports have made this clear. The arrival here, with Government backing, of numbers of Ismailis to take up land would give African politicians a most convenient stick with which to beat us. Nyerere and others would undoubtedly say that the fears of those [...] were fully justified. [...] However much we may sympathise with the plight of the Ismailis in South Africa, it would, we are convinced, be the height of political unwisdom at this particular time in our affairs to accede to the Aga Khan's request. [...]

Amusingly, an unknown civil servant has written the word 'Really!' by hand in the margin of this typed message, clearly disagreeing with the message. A subsequent internal Colonial Office memorandum[15] calls the response 'both discouraging and extremely disappointing.' In the same memorandum it is suggested that the Governor of Kenya is to be sounded out on accepting the Ismailis.

None of the above correspondence sheds any light as to the reason why the Ismailis were considered the least popular of all the Asians in Tanganyika, and the Colonial Office seems not to have made inquiries into the matter.

On 12 December, a letter[16] marked 'Confidential and Personal' was despatched to Sir Evelyn Baring, the Governor of Kenya, outlining the plight of the South African Ismailis and ending with the words: 'I do not think I need say more than this at present since I know that with your own South African experience and your knowledge of the Ismailis you will be looking at the Aga Khan's ideas as sympathetically as is possible within the limits set by your own political and economical difficulties. (Sgd.) W.L. Gorell Barnes.'

And indeed he did. On 24 March 1959, a letter[17] was sent by Alan Lennox-Boyd to the Aga Khan: '[...] I am glad to tell you that Sir Evelyn Baring has now written to say that he thinks it might be possible to arrange for the immigration of ten of these families, over a period of time to be settled when detailed arrangements are worked out. [...] I think I should add that the Governor is very anxious to avoid publicity over any arrangements which may be made, in case it gives grounds to other would-be immigrants [...] (Sgd.) Alan Lennox Boyd.' Just three days later, a letter[18] was received from the Aga Khan in reply:

My dear Alan, Thank you very much indeed for your letter of March 24th which I received on my arrival. I quite understand that the immigrant regulations for Kenya are strict, and that Sir Evelyn Baring does not want any publicity about Ismaili families moving from South Africa to Kenya. The President of the South Africa Ismaili Council, Count Keshavji, is capable and a good diplomat, and I am writing to him today giving him instructions as to what he can say and cannot say about the new East African immigrants. [...] Thank you very much again for the great help you have given me. I am sure that the Kenya Government will not have occasion to regret this move. I will write to Sir Evelyn Baring as you have suggested. (Sgd.) Much love from Mummy and happy Easter from both of us, as ever, K.

There followed considerable correspondence between the Governor of Kenya and the Colonial Office, resulting in a despatch[19] to the Aga Khan on 10 April 1959 by Alan Lennox-Boyd: '[...] Sir Evelyn Baring now tells me he hopes to be able to accept not only ten families in all, as I said in my letter to you of the 24th March, but forty families at a rate of about ten families a year. [...] I am sure that you will be as delighted with this news as I am. (Sgd.) Alan Lennox-Boyd.'

As his subsequent reply showed, the Aga Khan was indeed delighted. And well he might be. This most sensitive issue constituted the first test of the relationship between the Ismaili Muslims and the British Government since he assumed the Imamate. And the British response to the problem demonstrated beyond a shadow of a doubt that the special relationship between Britain and the Ismailis was alive and well.

A visit by the Aga Khan's uncle to the Gulf on behalf of the UN High Commissioner for Refugees

One of the sons of Aga Khan III, Prince Sadruddin Aga Khan, enjoyed a distinguished career[20] in international diplomacy. Serving in various high offices of the UN, he occupied the posts of United Nations High Commissioner for Refugees, UN coordinator for assistance to Afghanistan, and UN Executive Delegate in the Iraq-Turkey border areas. Although these activities generally fall outside the scope of this narrative, it can be noted that the official archives[21] show that the British government kept a discreet eye on his activities, while rendering some practical diplomatic assistance to support his activities. A report[22] from H.M. Political Agency in Kuwait, dated 9 July 1960, records:

The Prince was met at the Airport on arrival on June 14 by Shaikh Sa'ad al-Abdullah, Deputy President of the Police and Public Security Department, by a member of the Agency staff and by the whole of Kuwait's Ismaili Jama'at of about 150 persons. He called on the Ruler and the Political Agent the next morning, having previously asked for advice from a member of the Agency staff on methods of putting his case to His Highness. [...] The Ruler received him well but said he needed time to think the matter over before making a contribution to World Refugee Year. He said Kuwait had already contributed generously to the cause of the Algerian refugees. The Prince had to be content with this, and may be visiting us again.[...]

Some weeks later, a report[23] from the Political Agency in Kuwait reported the result of this visit, incidentally shedding an amusing light on the British view of the Kuwaiti ruler's public utterances:

You will probably have seen by now in the Press that the Ruler of Kuwait has contributed £40,000 to World Refugee Year. The news was put about here by Kuwait Radio in an announcement which added that His Highness had stipulated that the Palestinian and Algerian refugees should have first claim on the money; this is probably a gloss. [...] The Prince's visit to the Gulf has thus been remarkably successful.

No doubt this successful mission did no harm to Sadruddin Aga Khan's application for the position of High Commissioner for Refugees when this high office became available in later years. What is significant is that he turned directly to Britain's diplomatic representatives in the Gulf for assistance, and that this assistance was readily given. This episode bears out the ongoing bond between the Ismailis and Britain.

The Ismaili community in Uganda

As we saw in a previous paragraph, the Ismaili movement, widely dispersed geographically, on occasions found it necessary to withdraw its members from countries where the political climate became unfavourably disposed towards them. In 1960, such an event overtook the community in Uganda. It is recorded in the official archives[24] of the Dominions Office.

A telegram[25] to the Commonwealth Relations Office, dated 30 September 1960, communicated the concern of the Aga Khan for his comparatively large community in Uganda:

When dining with me last night [...] Prince Karim Aga Khan expressed concern about the future of his community in Uganda (which he estimates at about 15% of the population), and said that he would be grateful to have [...] advice. [...] The Aga Khan said that in spite of the trade boycott against Asians which had been going on for the past year he had not advised the community to leave Uganda. Ismaili money was still being invested there. Now however there were signs that East Africa was becoming a primary communist target and he feared that if the Kabaka (whom he obviously distrusts) "turned sour" a nasty Congo type situation might develop. He wonders whether in these circumstances he ought to advise members of his community to pull out.

A telegram[26] from the Commonwealth Relations Office to 'Karachi', which presumably meant the British High Commission there, gave rather unhelpful and somewhat nebulous advice in the matter:

Aga Khan must, of course, decide for himself whether to advise Ismailis to pull out of Uganda. You should, however, assure him that we should deplore their departure. Asian community have important part to play in maintaining economic stability on which progress of constitutional advance largely depends, and which we shall certainly do our best to maintain. [...] Danger that east Africa will become Communist targets obviously exists. You may, however, say that we do not believe Communists will be able in near future to make appreciable impact in Uganda, or that Kabaka is likely to join hands with them. [...] Colonial Secretary emphasised that absence of electoral safeguards for non-African communities in no way implied any relaxation of determination of United Kingdom Government to ensure adequate protection for all persons, of whatever race or creed, who had made their homes in Protectorate.

There followed some statements on HM Government's hope that stability would follow Uganda's independence. Thus the government committed itself to nothing and gave little helpful advice to the Aga Khan in the matter. The archive contains a number of such friendly, hopeful statements from Britain to the Aga Khan concerning the deteriorating situation of Ismailis (and indeed all Asians) in Uganda in 1960. The hard truth eventually led to the withdrawal of the Ismailis from Uganda. They now make up the larger proportion of the Ismaili community in London. It is not clear from the archives what support was given by Her Majesty's Government in their immigration to Britain and their eventual successful resettlement.

The Aga Khan hospital in Kenya

The Colonial Office records contain a small file[27] of correspondence from 1963 regarding a hospital in Kenya which enjoyed the support of the Aga Khan. This sheds an interesting light on the practical constraints affecting the relationship between Britain and the Ismailis at the time.

In a letter[28] dated 12 February 1963, the Aga Khan pleads for support to Duncan Sandys, Secretary of State for Commonwealth Relations:

My dear Mr Sandys, [...] Unfortunately on 20th October last, the African Medical and Research Foundation wrote to me saying that they could no longer consider meeting their share of the cost of the cancer treatment centre to be attached to the Aga Khan Hospital in Nairobi. This was a severe blow as well as being personally embarrassing, because I had already made a number of commitments about the centre and had succeeded in interesting a number of charitable organisations in the project. As a result of its decision I have resigned from the Honorary Chairmanship of the Foundation.

It is outside the scope of this book to investigate the reasons for this change of heart by the Foundation, but it makes for interesting speculation whether this was related in some way to the emerging African nationalism and conflicts surrounding the Ismaili communities in Africa. What is clear is that it underlines the Aga Khan's commitment to providing healthcare to his followers and the wider society. He continues:

The cost is much too heavy to be borne only by my community and myself and our first object must be to extend the present institution. I understand that the matter of the Kenya Government's grant for the extension of the hospital was referred by the Kenya Council of Ministers to a sub-Committee for further investigations. [...] I hope you will excuse me for bringing up the matter again, but I would be immensely grateful for any help you could give me in seeing that the Kenya Government does meet its promise of a further capital grant for the extension of the hospital. [...] Immense efforts have gone into making this institution a first class non-racial hospital, and I would be extremely distressed to see the institution suffer a very severe set-back. [...] Preliminary contacts have been established with German and Swiss banking and industrial circles, and the initial response has been very favourable.

Thus, the Aga Khan felt free to enlist the help of London officialdom in achieving an altogether noble aim. Furthermore, the letter also illustrates the *modus operandi* of the Aga Khan in such circumstances: rather than relying solely on direct payment from the Ismaili movement towards such a healthcare institution, he sought to engage his network to achieve other forms of financing. It could not be ascertained from the British archives how far these financing efforts were successful. However, his appeal to Duncan Sandys did trigger some consideration by the Government of Kenya, as evidenced by a memorandum[29] from the Governor's Office dated 14 March 1963, which declared: 'The sub-committee reviewed the facts and reached the conclusion that there was a moral obligation on the Government to make the grant. [...] The subcommittee further concluded, however, that the Government was in no position, in its present financial state, to honour this obligation.'

An interesting dilemma for the colonial authorities to conjure with, especially in the light of their often stated desire to remain on friendly terms with the Aga Khan, and the evident nobility of the cause for which he has appealed to them. However, the memorandum goes on to show that practical constraints won the day:

The sub-committee accordingly recommend that the Minister for Finance [of the Kenya colonial government, MvG] should be asked to raise the matter [...] in discussion with the Aga Khan, and to explain to him, frankly and forthrightly, that, while the Government acknowledges that a moral commitment was enter into on its behalf in 1960, it is in a condition of extreme financial stringency which virtually precludes its meeting that commitment within the foreseeable future. He should invite the Aga Khan to release the Government from its obligation, preferably wholly, but, failing that, to the extent of reducing the sum involved as much as possible and accepting payment of the reduced sum over a period of, say, five years.

The Aga Khan's response is not recorded in the file, but the news must have been a personal disappointment to him when it was conveyed. There is no hint of London coming to the rescue financially in this matter. And thus we see illustrated, to some extent, the practical limits of mutual support rendered between Britain and the Ismailis under such circumstances.

The issue of passports for stateless Ismaili children

The British official archives contain a voluminous and rather legalistic file[30] concerning a request from the Aga Khan to issue British passports to stateless Ismaili children. The correspondence in the file sheds a further interesting light on the attitude of British officialdom to the Aga Khan's more unusual and legally sensitive requests.

A memorandum[31] from Sir Edward Peck KCMG of the Foreign and Commonwealth Office, dated 5 March 1969, records:

H.H. the Aga Khan called on me on 28 February to discuss the possibilities of providing United Kingdom passports for certain stateless children of United Kingdom nationals belonging to the Ismaili sect. [...] Although he said the numbers were not large, the Aga Khan mentioned a figure of 400 Zanzibaris (not, however, resident in Tanzania), and said there were other groups—e.g. in Kuwait, Rwanda, Burundi, and the Malagasy Republic. [...] There was no precedent for doing this in the sort of case or for such numbers as the Aga Khan had in mind. The latter asked, however, that the Secretary of State be urged to consider his request sympathetically.

The latter sentence is typical of responses to those requests made by the Aga Khan to the British Government, allowing them freedom of action while clearly requesting positive support in meeting or facilitating his requests. The memorandum continues: 'He said that he was prepared to give a personal guarantee that none of those to whom passports were given would ever try to settle in the United Kingdom and that if they were expelled from their present countries of residence he would arrange their resettlement elsewhere.'

It would be very interesting to investigate whether any of the people concerned did, in spite of the Aga Khan's promise, ever end up in the United Kingdom. This falls outside the scope of this book; in addition, the immigration files dealing with the mass expulsions of Ismailis from African countries and their eventual resettlement in Britain and elsewhere in later years are not yet available for inspection. However, it is clear from this remark that the Aga Khan saw a clear threat of expulsion for a number of his communities around the world, but also felt he had such influence over their actions that he could promise the authorities in London that they would not settle in the United Kingdom. The memorandum continues: '[...] The Aga Khan is a serious and dedicated young man who has his people's interests very much at heart, and I therefore consider that his request deserves very serious and sympathetic consideration, and that if it is at all possible for us to help him in this matter we should do so.'

Some months later, the issue was again brought up by the Aga Khan when he met with Sir Edward Peck, as shown by a memorandum[32] dated 19 September 1969: 'The Aga Khan called on me yesterday. Sir Stanley Tomlinson and Mr Webb of Nationality and Treaty Department were present. [...] Should we be able to do something for the children concerned we should, in conveying our decision to His Highness, make it clear that the concession depends on there being no other candidates apart from those whose particulars he has furnished.'

So it is evident that the Foreign and Commonwealth Office was prepared to support the Aga Khan's request, but at the same time tried to contain the issue and would not allow it to become a permanently standing arrangement. The memorandum then sheds some interesting light on the situation of the Ismailis in the Congo: 'The Aga Khan expressed his appreciation of the vigorous efforts being made by our Chargé d'Affaires at Kinshasa and our consular officers in the Congo on behalf of those members of the Ismaili community for whose protection they are responsible, and asked that this might be conveyed to the Chargé d'Affaires. By contrast the Tanzanian Ambassador, a Zanzibari, would not lift a finger to help Tanzanian nationals.'

The memorandum then addresses the expulsion decisions announced in Congo around that time, and adds:

The Aga Khan asked if we knew what was behind the expulsion decision. He of course recognised that there were many people of doubtful honesty among the foreign communities in the Congo, the Ismaili community not excepted. [...] On being asked whether I thought there was any hope of the Congolese being led to reverse their policy on expulsion, I said that I thought this was too much to hope for but that the representation made might succeed in obtaining a respite for some of the Asians and East Africans. His Highness asked whether in that case I would recommend his people to contemplate remaining in the Congo or to make plans to leave after obtaining the best price they could for their businesses, etc. I said that because of the extreme difficulty of forecasting events in the Congo even as much as a week ahead, I would be hesitant to make any recommendations. I gave a similar answer about the Congo's future.

Thus, in that time of trial and tribulation for his people in the Congo, the Aga Khan again turned to Britain for an appraisal of the situation and for assistance in the form of quite diplomacy. The British civil service machine then went into operation to provide the requested passports, as evidenced by a memorandum[33] from the Nationality and Treaty department dated 25 September 1969: 'He [the Aga Khan, MvG] was told that while the issue of United Kingdom passports to such people would present difficulties we would certainly give it sympathetic consideration if he would provide us with details from which we could assess the size of the problem. His Highness has now done this.'

There followed lengthy interdepartmental correspondence about the legality and practicability of this move, and on measures to prevent this support for the Ismailis from becoming a precedent for others who might wish to avail themselves of a British passport. A short internal note[34] from Mr Webb of the Nationality and Treaty Department to Sir Edward Peck, dated 8 October 1969, asked: 'Do you wish to write to the Aga Khan saying that the necessary consultations are in hand? If so, I will draft.' Most interestingly, this note was returned to Mr Webb the following day, with a handwritten comment: 'Could you rapidly do so? This would be an occasion to congratulate him on his engagement and keep the dialogue going. (Sgd) E.P. 9/10.'

This little handwritten note again confirms the desire of senior British officialdom to remain on close terms with the Aga Khan, keep communication channels open, and retain the special relationship between Britain and the Ismailis. The files are inconclusive as to the eventual outcome and the actual implementation of Britain's desire to help the Aga Khan in this matter. However, they contain a handwritten letter[35] from the Aga Khan, dated 20 October 1969, with which this chapter of the narrative can conveniently be concluded:

Dear Sir Edward, Thank you so much for your letter of the 15th October [...]. I hope that sympathetic consideration will be given to the cases of the Ismailis of Kuwait and look forward to hearing from you in due course. The news I have been receiving from the Congo tallies well with your information and I can but hope that if discreet but continuous pressure is exercised, the Congolese Government will adopt a more rational and understanding attitude. The numbers involved in the case of the Ismaili community are so small that I can hardly see how they would have any effect, apart perhaps from the matter being one of principle. Lastly, but by no means least, thank you very much indeed for your congratulations and wishes on the occasion of my engagement. I am much looking forward to having a wife and I hope a family, and also hope that when we are next in England, I will be able to introduce my wife to you. Yours sincerely, Aga Khan.

And thus the special relationship between the Aga Khan and senior British officials, and between the Ismaili Muslims and Britain, was alive and well in 1969. The Aga Khan looked forward to raising a family, but had no reason to doubt that he was closely aligned with, and indeed a welcome part of, the close knit and warm family which makes up the British establishment.

Conclusions

In the last years of the Imamate of Aga Khan III, the British Government took a favourable view of the activities and socio-political attitude of the Ismailis in Pakistan and East Africa in 1955. Subsequently, in the first years of the Imamate of Aga Khan IV, the British Government undertook considerable efforts, and indeed ran some risks, in assisting the relocation of the Ismaili community of South Africa to Kenya. In doing so, it gave active support and preferential treatment to the Ismailis, thereby reaffirming the Ismaili-British relationship which had existed during the Imamate of Aga Khan III. Both parties undertook this engagement in conditions of strict confidentiality, thereby demonstrating a considerable degree of mutual trust.

In 1960, the British diplomatic representation in Kuwait gave practical diplomatic support to the fundraising activities of Prince Sadruddin Aga Khan on behalf of the UNHCR, thereby illustrating the bond between the Ismaili leadership and Britain at that time; but the British Government in that same year steered clear of giving clear and unequivocal advice to the Aga Khan regarding the withdrawal of the Ismaili community of Uganda.

In 1969, the Aga Khan requested passport facilities for stateless Ismaili children. This request was given 'sympathetic consideration' in spite of legal difficulties and the significant risk of creating an undesirable precedent. From that sympathetic response it is clear that the relationship between the Aga Khan and his followers on the one hand, and Britain on the other, was indeed on a very positive and exclusive basis at the time.

9

CONCLUSIONS

From the totality of the material examined in this book, it may be concluded that the Ismaili Muslims constitute a modern, socio-economically successful temporal and religious movement. They are without a doubt a movement with Islamic origins and an Islamic self-image. Nevertheless, this image is contested by many voices from within mainstream Islam.

It has been demonstrated that the movement is strongly aligned with British interests, derives its temporal status from Britain, and can count on British diplomatic and (semi)official support. The link between the successive Aga Khans and the British Government has its origins in the 'Great Game', when both parties commenced the cultivation of mutually friendly relations. As a result, the leadership of the Ismaili movement, in the person of Aga Khan III, rendered vital assistance to Britain in the First World War, and exercised a moderating influence on Muslims throughout the British Empire in the 1920s and 1930s. Subsequently, continuous mutual assistance was rendered between Britain and the Ismailis, although this was rarely if ever in the public eye.

Britain played a key role in enabling the modernization and transformation of the movement, and in establishing and enabling centralised control over the movement by Aga Khan III and Aga Khan IV. The modernity of the movement, and its alignment with British interest, are the product of enlightened Ismaili leadership, intertwined with a careful nurturing of the movement and its leadership by the British colonial and imperial governments, over a period of more than a century. The British civil service has been the key agent, and the key element of continuity, on the British side in this evolving relationship.

Indeed, the process of modernization owes much to the continuity of policy and behaviour as embodied by the actions of the civil service, especially since that service contributed in no small measure to maintaining stable and mutually beneficial relations between Britain and the Ismaili movement over a comparatively long period which saw many a change of government and political direction in Britain, and indeed saw the sudden and turbulent end of the British Empire.

From the material examined, it is evident that the nurturing of the British-Ismaili relationship took place for the most part outside the domain of public politics, and was not subject to public scrutiny. Nor did the relationship develop overnight. Through a careful process of give-and-take, the bonds were continuously, indeed inexorably, formed. On occasions one side disappointed the other, or did not take desired actions. There were moments of mutual irritation, and indeed on occasions there were misplaced expectations by one party. But systematically, such failings were overlooked and the relationship was mutually deemed important enough to survive.

Both parties had significant credit with each other, but that credit was not unlimited: although Britain repeatedly intervened on behalf of the Ismailis when their interests were threatened, and remained prepared to consider taking action, it was not a permanent agent acting on behalf of the Ismaili movement. Most requests for assistance were carefully weighed, and tested against the limits of practical do-ability and realism. Nor was Britain prepared to give its unconditional and perpetual endorsement to the Ismaili leadership. The bestowal of temporal status, and practical support, was made dependent on the allegiance and attitude of the Ismaili movement and its leadership.

We set out on this research, as mentioned in the introduction, in order to attempt to find an answer to the question whether there are any Muslim communities to be found in modern Britain which remain to all intents and purposes integrated in British society or co-opted to further key British interests; and if so, how this integration or co-optation has come about.

The key conclusions from the perspective of a student of Islam, a sociologist, a diplomat or the leader of an Islamic movement must be that it is possible to achieve the modernization of an Islamic movement, and indeed its alignment and co-optation with 'The Western Way' as embodied by Western ideals of modernity and a Western view of the world. However, it is outside the powers of the author of this book to rule on whether such a development is actually desirable. That will depend on an individual and collective perspective, and will be heavily influenced by the cultural and religious background, and indeed the scientific perspective or practical and ideological objectives of the readership. Nor can the author rule on the question whether the Ismaili movement has lost its credentials as an Islamic movement through its cooptation by the British. That too will depend on political, philosophical and theological opinion, and indeed on individual opinions of the role which a movement such as the Ismaili movement may or may not be allowed to play in the world.

Our examination of the evolving British-Ismaili relationship does demonstrate that alignment and mutual co-optation are indeed possible, but also that they require the painstaking building of trust, over a prolonged period of time. There must be a degree of willingness among the leadership of a movement to be co-opted, and this willingness must be carefully and patiently nurtured in key individuals. There must be a party outside the movement, in this case the British Government, which has both the vision and the ability to recognise the potential for cooptation, and which possesses the skills, empathy and resources to nurture the relationship as it develops. This requires continuity of vision, continuity of purpose, and the absence of a desire for 'quick wins' or short-term goals. The Ismailis found such a partner in the British civil service and colonial administration which, although acting in the name of the Government, were in practice neither bound nor constrained by short-term political objectives and electoral agendas, nor subject to penetrating public scrutiny.

It is interesting to note that the relationship between Britain and the Ismailis seems to have grown on the basis of services mutually rendered, many of which were comparatively small, and none of which seems to have involved a direct transaction. The movement was not bought, nor was Britain contracted by the Ismailis to do its bidding on the world stage. Rather, on the basis of practical actions which were within the realm of the possible and realistic, both parties gradually helped each other to strengthen their respective position. The Aga Khan gained temporal status. Britain gained a friend well-disposed towards the Empire. The Aga Khan gained a high degree of control over his movement. Britain gained a worldwide network. The Aga Khan became a statesman. Britain gained a valuable set of eyes and ears in the Muslim world.

Therein may be found a number of key lessons. It must be questioned whether a similar relationship between an Islamic movement and a Western Government might come to fruition in today's world of quick fixes and short-term agendas. All too often, short-term solutions are sought for long-term problems, usually in the full glare of the media, to satisfy short-term political necessities and respond to the electoral cycles of modern democracy.

For such a relationship to flourish, a degree of discretion and an even higher degree of wisdom are required from both parties. Britain did not advertise its involvement in the inner workings of the Ismaili movement, but it certainly was involved in the key decisions surrounding the appointment of Aga Khan IV as Imam of the Nizari Ismailis. And these decisions may be said to have a significant religious and spiritual dimension, as well as a temporal and worldly element, the nature of which was directly influenced by Britain. This crucial involvement further illustrates the need for wisdom and skill in developing such a delicate relationship: the need for a judicious involvement where strictly necessary, whilst at all times avoiding the kind of dominant involvement which might draw the Government into petty internal squabbles and the type of human issues that exist in every movement. The British Government acted wisely in this instance by taking only those actions necessary for stability and continuity, and by acting in such a way that the continued loyalty of the Ismailis could be ensured. It was able to do so because the world did not know it was involved.

One particular incident in the evolving relationship which we examined sheds a crucial light on the indirect benefits which may result from such an arrangement, and the forces to which it is subjected. The Aga Khan's assessment of the Turkish peace settlement upon the conclusion of the First World War showed that he saw, with amazing clarity, what few appeared to see at the time: a troubled Middle East and Asia, and Islam at war with itself. Although it was recognised for the valuable advice that it was by the civil servants who were directly involved with the Aga Khan, the warning was not heeded by the politically appointed delegates to the peace conference. Many of these delegates, it may be surmised, had a series of short-term objectives to fulfil. But think of what might have been if his advice had been heeded in those heady days. We shall never know for certain, but no one can doubt the fact that the British obtained a piece of advice which was given from a unique perspective and a unique background. Herein lies another one of the positive potential benefits of a relationship such as that which we have examined.

Will we ever see another such case of mutual alignment and co-optation? The development of a similar special relationship elsewhere is difficult to imagine as it is dependent on the structures and organization of the religious and temporal authority within the movement or group concerned.

But those who are charged with cultivating relations across one of the great divides of our time would do well to heed the lessons of the carefully nurtured relationship between Britain and the global Ismaili community.

10

RECOMMENDATIONS FOR FURTHER RESEARCH

A certain type of documentation was absent from the myriad official archives that were explored during the research for this book. This raises a number of interesting questions, as well as potential opportunities for further research. Among the topics missing from the archive are the following:

a) Any official British description of the specific services rendered by Aga Khan I during the Afghan War, and the wider Great Game in the 1840s.

b) Any mention of specific activities by the worldwide Ismaili community during the Great War, which one might conceivably have expected based on the Aga Khan's exhortations to support the Empire.

c) Any report of Ismaili life and activities in German- and Japanese-occupied territories during the Second World War, and their contact with the Aga Khan (if indeed any such contact were possible).

This absence of documentary material may be explained by a number of factors, quite conceivably working in conjunction, such as the loss of records, chaotic record-keeping in times of crisis, incomplete information received in London during the time of the East India Company's rule of India, and other such mundane causes. Alternatively, some of the gaps in documentation may be explained by the fact that highly sensitive documentation may be held for up to a century. Therefore, it is reasonable to assume that some of the more sensitive material concerning Ismaili activities during the First and the Second World War is not yet available for inspection, if indeed it exists. It is conceivable that this material may have been deliberately destroyed. However, key areas for suggested future research are:

a) Formal records regarding the earliest support given by Aga Khan I and the Ismailis to Britain. It is conceivable that there are existing archives in India and Pakistan, formerly the property of either the East India Company or the British Indian government, which may have been created at the time, and were left behind at Independence.

b) Specific intelligence-gathering or other such activities by the Ismaili movement during the Great War. If indeed this material is covered by the 100–year secrecy classification, it should be released in the period 2014 to 2019.

c) The life of the Ismaili communities in German- and Japanese-occupied territories during the Second World War, and their contact with the Aga Khan, if any such contact was possible. Quite possibly, German and Japanese archives regarding the administration of occupied territories might contain some references to the community, to the extent that these archives still exist.

NOTES

PREFACE

1. James Masselos, "The Khojas of Bombay: The defining of formal membership criteria during the nineteenth century" in Imtiaz Ahmad, *Caste and Social Stratification Among the Muslims* (Delhi: Manohar, 1973), pp. 1–20.
2. Hamid Algar, "The revolt of the Agha Khan Mahallati and the transference of the Ismaili Imamate to India", *Studia Islamica*, XIX, 1969, pp. 55–81.
3. Amrita Shodhan, *A Question of Community: Religious Groups in Colonial India* (Calcutta: Somaiya, 2001).
4. Aga Khan, *The Memoirs of the Aga Khan: World Enough and Time* (London: Cassell and Co., 1954), pp. 179–182.
5. While there exists no census of the world's Ismailis, their centres of population (the Northern Areas of Pakistan, Tajikistan's Gorno-Badakshan Autonomous Oblast and Afghan Badakshan) cannot account for more than half a million persons. Adding to these the more modest numbers in China, India, Iran, Syria, Tanzania, Kenya and Uganda, as well as those who have emigrated more recently to Europe and North America, provides us with a generous estimate of a few millions.
6. For a study of the Aga Khan's religious and political views see Michel Boivin, *La Rénovation du Shî'isme Ismaélien en Inde et au Pakistan* (London: Routledge Curzon, 2003).
7. Paul Kaiser, *Culture, Transnationalism, and Civil Society: Aga Khan Social Service Initiatives in Tanzania* (London: Praeger, 1996).
8. H.S. Morris, *The Indians in Uganda: Caste and Sect in a Plural Society* (London: Weidenfeld and Nicolson, 1968).
9. Azim Nanji, "Modernization and change in the Nizari Ismaili Community in East Africa", *Journal of Religion in Africa*, vol. 6, no. 2 (1974), pp. 123–139.
10. To my knowledge there is no scholarly work on these movements, though they produce many printed works and electronic publications. Among the many books of the most eminent of these charismatic leaders, see for

111

instance a collection of one hundred questions and answers about various theological matters by Nasir al-Din Hunzai, *Sau Sawal* (Karachi: Khana-e Hikmat, 1978).

1. INTRODUCTION AND OBJECTIVES

1. K. Deutsch, *Nationalism and Social Communication* (Harvard 1966).
2. M. Gladwell, *The Tipping Point* (London 2000).
3. D. Hinds, *Critical Mass Behaviour and Transaction Costs in Open Source and Open Content Projects* (Miami 2004).
4. Akbarally Meherally, *A History of the Agakhani Ismailis* (Burnaby, Can. 1991).

2. FROM 'ASSASSIN LEGENDS' TO MODEL CITIZENS: A BRIEF HISTORY OF THE ISMAILI MUSLIMS

1. F. Daftary, *The Ismailis: Their History and Doctrines* (Cambridge 1990); idem, *The Assassin Legends: Myths of the Ismailis* (New York 1995 and London 2001); B. Lewis, *The Assassins: a Radical Sect in Islam* (London 1967).
2. Daftary, *The Ismailis*, op. cit.; Lewis, *The Assassins*, op. cit.
3. Daftary, *The Ismailis*, op. cit.; idem, *The Assassin Legends*, op. cit.; Lewis, *The Assassins*, op. cit.
4. Daftary, *The Assassin Legends*, op. cit.; Lewis, *The Assassins*, op. cit..
5. F. Daftary, *Ismailis in Medieval Muslim Societies* (London and New York 2005).
6. P. Willey, *Eagle's Nest: Ismaili Castles in Iran and Syria* (London and New York 2005).
7. Daftary, *The Ismailis*, op. cit.; idem, *The Assassin Legends*, op. cit..
8. Lewis, *The Assassins*, op. cit.
9. Daftary, *The Assassin Legends*, op. cit.
10. Lewis, *The Assassins*, op. cit.
11. Daftary, *The Assassin Legends*, op. cit.
12. Willey, *Eagle's Nest*, op. cit.
13. Daftary, *The Ismailis*, op. cit.; Lewis, *The Assassins*, op. cit.
14. R. Stark and W.S. Bainbridge, *The Future of Religion* (New York 1985).
15. A. Nanji, 'Modernization and Change in the Nizari Ismaili Community in East Africa: A Perspective', *Journal of Religion in Africa*, Vol. 6 (1974).
16. P.B. Clarke, 'The Ismailis: A Study of Community', *The British Journal of Sociology*, Vol. 27 (1976).
17. Ibid.
18. Ibid.
19. Stark and Bainbridge, *The Future*, op. cit.
20. K.K. Aziz (ed.), *Selected Speeches and Writings of Sir Sultan Muhammad Shah* (London and New York 1998).

21. Private letter from Dr Kutub Kassam of the Institute of Ismaili Studies in London to the author.
22. Daftary, *The Ismailis* (n. 5).

3. FIRST CONTACT (1840–1914)

1. Obituary of Aga Khan III in *The Times*, dated 12 July 1957, contained in Dominions Office records, DO/35/5260, The National Archives, Kew.
2. Hamid Algar, 'The Revolt of Agha Khan Mahallati and the Transference of the Ismai'ili Imamate to India', *Studia Islamica*, Paris 1969.
3. A brief description of the role of Aga Khan I and II in Nizari Ismaili history, as represented on the Institute of Ismaili Studies website (London 2006).
4. Dominions Office records, DO 35/5260, The National Archives, Kew.
5. Colonial Office records, CO 822/1209, The National Archives, Kew.
6. P. Hopkirk, *The Great Game* (London 2006).
7. Obituary of Aga Khan III in *The Times*, dated 12 July 1957, contained in Dominions Office records, DO/35/5260, The National Archives, Kew.
8. India Office records, IOR/L/PJ/6/236 (file 1571), British Library, London.
9. Memorandum dated 24 June 1955, concerning a visit from the Aga Khan's legal adviser, Sir George Allen, to the Colonial Office, contained in Colonial Office records, CO 822/746, The National Archives, Kew.
10. Reuters Press Agency telegrams, dated Geneva 11 July 1957, contained in Dominions Office records, DO/35/5260, The National Archives, Kew.
11. Memorandum concerning a visit from the Aga Khan's legal adviser, op. cit.
12. Dominions Office records, DO 35/5260, The National Archives, Kew.
13. Aziz (ed.), *Selected Speeches and Writings*, op. cit.
14. 'Presidential address to the all India Muhammadan Educational Conference', Delhi, 1902, as quoted in ibid.
15. 'Budget speech in the Council of the Governor General, Calcutta', 25 March 1903; and 'Budget Speech in the Council of the Governor General', Calcutta, 30 March 1904, as quoted in ibid.
16. 'Speech at the Muslim educational conference', Bombay 1904, as quoted in ibid.
17. 'The memorial presented by a Muslim deputation to the Viceroy of India', Simla, 1 October 1906, as quoted in ibid.
18. Article in *The National Review*, London, February 1907, as quoted in ibid.
19. 'Inaugural address to the Deccan Muslim League meeting', Poona, 12 August 1908, as quoted in ibid.
20. Interview with *The Times*, 14 February 1909, as quoted in ibid.
21. 'Speech at a meeting held to protest against the treatment of Indians in South Africa', Bombay, 10 December 1913, as quoted in ibid.
22. Gladwell, *The Tipping Point*, op. cit.

4. CRISIS YEARS: 'MUCH VALUABLE SERVICE' (1914–1920)

1. R.K. Massie, *Dreadnought: Britain, Germany and the Coming of the First World War* (New York 1998); idem, *Castles of Steel: Britain, Germany and the Winning of the Great War at Sea* (New York 2003).

2. P. Hopkirk, *On Secret Service East of Constantinople: the Plot to Bring down the British Empire* (London 1994 and 2006), chapter 2, 'Deutschland über Allah!'

3. 'The Indian Muslim outlook', article in *The Edinburgh Review*, as quoted in Aziz (ed.), *Selected Speeches and Writings*, op. cit.

4. Reuters Press Agency telegrams, 11 July 1957, op. cit.

5. Obituary of Aga Khan III in *The Times*, op. cit.

6. 'Speech at a meeting of the Indian volunteers committee', London, 1 October 1914, as quoted in Aziz (ed.), *Selected Speeches and Writings* (n. 24).

7. The 1914–1918 Forum [website] >www.1914–1918.net.dlgs_speech.htm<, accessed on 9 October 2006.

8. [Note: the author of this book considers it unfortunate that the original text of this speech could not be recovered from either The National Archives, Kew or the British Library, London. This may be explained by the fact that such political speeches were (and are) frequently written shortly before the meetings at which they are delivered, and subsequently discarded. If such a speech has not been prepared through official channels, but rather by the speaker itself, either on paper or by speaking 'off-the-cuff', it is highly unlikely to have been preserved as an official document. Hence, we must represent it here as recovered from a secondary source.]

9. File marked 'Confidential: Closed Until 1966', and entitled 'Memorandum of a conversation Rt Hon Austen Chamberlain and Aga Khan about Indian contribution to war loan', contained in Chancellery of the Exchequer records, T172/238, The National Archives, Kew.

10. A handwritten letter, dated July 1915, on personal stationery headed '9 Egerton Place S.W.' to the Chancellor of the Exchequer from Austen Chamberlain, contained in Chancellery of the Exchequer records (n. 56).

11. A typed memorandum of a conversation between Austen Chamberlain and the Aga Khan, undated, contained in ibid.

12. P. Hopkirk, *On Secret Service*, chapter 2, op. cit.

13. 'Message to the Indian Muslims on Turkish Entry into the War', London, 2 November 1914, published in *The Times*, 4 November 1914, as quoted in ibid.

14. Colonial Office records, CO 323/644, The National Archives, Kew.

15. Obituary of Aga Khan III in *The Times*, op. cit.

16. Additional obituary of Aga Khan III in *The Times*, dated 12 July 1957, contained in Dominions Office records, DO/35/5260, The National Archives, Kew.

17. A file entitled 'Views of the Aga Khan on proposed Turkish settlement', dated 1920, contained in Foreign Office records, RO 608/272, The National Archives, Kew.

18. A typed letter, dated 8 January 1920 and headed 'Atlantic Hotel, Nice', from the Aga Khan to E.S. Montagu, contained in ibid.

19. A typed letter, dated 13 January 1920, from E.S. Montagu to (unidentified) colleagues, contained in ibid.

20. Memorandum from the Foreign and Political department, Government of India, Simla, 5 January 1920, contained in India Office Records, IOR/R/1/1/853, British Library, London.

5. INTERBELLUM: FROM STAUNCH ALLY TO 'A BROKEN REED' (1920–1939)

1. 'Message to the East India Association, Paris', 17 June 1928, as quoted in Aziz (ed.), *Selected Speeches and Writings*, op. cit.

2. Article in *The Times*, 12 and 13 October 1928, as quoted in ibid.

3. Interview with *The Times of India*, 28 December 1928, as quoted in ibid.

4. Letter to *The Times*, published on 18 January 1930, as quoted in ibid.

5. Obituary of Aga Khan III in *The Times*, op. cit.

6. Letter to Sir Stewart Symes KCMG KBE DSO, dated 23 December 1932, contained in Colonial Office records, CO 822/47/11, The National Archives, Kew.

7. Aziz (ed.), *Selected Speeches and Writings* (n. 24); letter to *The Times* on the Hindu-Muslim problem in India, London, 7 June 1932.

8. Letter from Aga Khan III to Sir Philip Cunliffe-Lister GBE PC, dated 21 December 1932, contained in Colonial Office records, op. cit.

9. Correspondence between the Deputy Governor of Uganda and the Secretary of State for the Colonies, contained in Colonial Office records, CO 536/181/3, The National Archives, Kew.

10. Ibid.

11. Letter (preserved in draft form) from Sir Cecil Bottomley at the Colonial Office to Sir Bernard Bourdillon KBE KCMG, dated 13 March 1934, contained in ibid.

12. Letter (preserved in draft form) from Lord Plymouth, on behalf of the Secretary of State for the Colonies, to the Governor of Uganda, dated 14 March 1934, contained in ibid.

13. P. Hopkirk, *Setting the East Ablaze: Lenin's Dream of an Empire in Asia* (New York and London 1984).

14. Letter marked 'Very Secret' from the Foreign and Political Department at Simla to J.C. Walton CB MC at the India Office in Whitehall, dated 20 July 1933, contained in India Office Records, IOR/L/PS/12/3186, British Library, London.

15. A copy of memorandum No. 474 dated 15 April 1933, from the Assistant Political Agent, Chitral, to the Political Agent, Dir, Swat and Chitral. Attached to, op. cit.

16. A letter marked 'Confidential' from Lt-Col. J.W. Thomson Glover CBE, His Britannic Majesty's Consul General, Kashgar, to the Foreign Secretary to the Government of India, dated 28 March 1935, contained in ibid.

17. A typed set of minutes of the Political Department of the Government of India, (by hand) dated 22 June; from position in the file, and reference to other documents, these were written in 1935. Contained in ibid.

18. A letter marked 'Very Secret' from the Foreign and Political Department at Simla to J.C. Walton CB MC at the India Office in Whitehall, dated 7 August 1935, contained in ibid.

19. Undated typed note with handwritten short comments. The handwritten comments are dated 29.8 and 27.8.35. Attached to ibid.

20. Intelligence report from an unidentified source, dated 27 August 1935, contained in ibid.

21. A letter from the Colonial Office, addressed to A. de V. Wade Esq CMG OBE, dated 9 November 1936, contained in Colonial Office records, CO 822/70/18, The National Archives, Kew.

22. Correspondence regarding the 'relations between the Sultan of Muscat and the followers of Aga Khan in that territory', contained in India Office Records, IOR/L/PS/12/28J, British Library, London.

23. Letter dated 7 April 1939 from Aga Khan III to A.C.B. Symon, India Office, London, as contained in ibid.

24. A typed internal memo of the Colonial Office from A.C.B. Symon to a Mr Walton, dated 14 April 1939, contained in ibid.

25. Handwritten response from Mr Walton to A.C.B. Symon on a typed Colonial Office internal memo, dated 14 April 1939, contained in ibid.

26. Typed letter from Mr A.C.B. Symon, written on neutral stationery in a private capacity, to H.H. The Rt Hon Aga Khan PC GCSI GCIE GCVO, dated 18 April 1939, contained in ibid.

27. Typed letter from the Aga Khan to A.C.B. Symon Esq at the India Office, London, dated 21 April 1939, contained in ibid.

28. Typed letter from A.C.B. Symon, written on neutral stationery in a private capacity, to H.H. The Rt Hon Aga Khan PC GCSI GCIE GCVO, dated 25 April 1939, contained in ibid.

29. Copy of a typed letter, dated 21 April 1939 and marked 'Private and Personal', to Sir H.A.F. Metcalfe KCIE CSI MVO, Government of India, External Affairs Department, which appears to be signed by R.T. Peel MC of the India Office, contained in ibid.

30. A letter, dated Simla, 2 May 1939, marked 'Private and Personal', from Sir H.A.F. Metcalfe of the External Affairs Department of the Government of India, to R.T. Peel Esq MC, of the India Office, London, contained in ibid.

31. A letter dated 7 June 1939, marked 'personal', from T.C. Fowle at the Residency, Bushire, to Sir Aubery Metcalfe KCIE CSI MVO, Secretary to the Government of India, External Affairs Department, Simla, contained in ibid.

32. A short report dated 19 June 1939, sent by T. Hickinbotham of the British Consulate and Political Agency, Muscat to the Hon'ble Lt Col Sir Trenchard Fowle KCIE CBE, Political Resident in the Persian Gulf, Bushire, added (as a copy) to a letter from T. Fowle to Sir Aubrey Metcalfe KCIE CSI MVO, Secretary to the Government of India, External Affairs Department, and contained in ibid.

33. Copy of a letter sent by H.A.F. Metcalfe, dated 20 July 1939, and headed 'External Affairs Department, Simla', addressed to Aga Khan III at his Villa Jane Andrées at Cap Antibes, France, contained in ibid.

34. A file regarding the 'Social status of Prince Ali Khan, (son of H.H. the Aga Khan) and his wife', dated 1939, and marked 'Closed until 1990', contained in Colonial Office records, CO 533/414/11, The National Archives, Kew.

35. A letter marked 'confidential' and dated 7 March 1939, to the Right Honourable Malcolm MacDonald MP, Secretary of State for the Colonies, Downing Street, London, from the Governor's deputy, Government House, Nairobi, Kenya, contained in ibid.

36. A letter marked 'confidential' and dated 31 March 1939, to Mr J.J. Paskin Esq, the India Office, Whitehall, from the India Office (signature of the sender is illegible), contained in ibid.

37. Copy of a letter marked 'confidential, Kenya' and dated 14 April 1939 to the Governor of Kenya, Air Chief Marshal Sir Robert Brooke-Popham, from the Colonial Office, Downing Street, London (signature of sender illegible), contained in ibid.

6. WAR CLOUDS AGAIN (1939–1953)

1. Obituary of Aga Khan III in *The Times*, op.cit.

2. Letter, dated 24 October 1939, sent by Aga Khan III from Hotel Ritz, Place Vendome, Paris to the Most Hon. Marquess of Zetland, Secretary of State for India, London, contained in records of the Ministry of Agriculture, Fisheries and Food, MAF 121/148, The National Archives, Kew.

3. Undated draft of a letter (referring to report in chapter 5, note 32), to Sir Eric Machtig KCMG OBE; undated draft of a letter, referring to India Office Records, to Sir Alan Barlow KBE CB; both in Ministry of Agriculture, Fisheries and Foods records, op.cit.

4. Obituary of Aga Khan III in *The Times*, op.cit.

5. A memo from G.R. Woodward, referenced 'Th 21385', dated 11 February 1955, contained in records of the Ministry of Agriculture, Fisheries and Food, op.cit.

6. A file dated 1952, and entitled 'War Damage Compensation Claims against French Gov't by Aga Khan and Aly Khan', contained in Foreign Office records, FO/146/4610, The National Archives, Kew.

7. A typed letter date 14 February 1945, from the British Embassy in Paris to the Foreign Office, contained in ibid.

8. An inward telegram, dated 16 February 1945, from H.M. Consul General at Nice to His Majesty's Ambassador, Paris, contained ibid.

9. An outgoing (undated) reply-telegram (replying to letter referred to in note 83), from H.M. Ambassador, Paris to the British Consul, Nice, contained in ibid.

10. A telegram, date illegible (but calculated as 3 January 1946 from letter in note 108), from the Aga Khan to the Foreign Office, contained ibid.

11. A typed letter, dated 18 January 1946, from H.L. Rabino, Consul General in charge of War Damages Department, to the Aga Khan, contained in ibid.

12. A typed letter from the Ministère des Affaires Etrangères, Direction des Affaires Economiques et Financières, Paris to the British Embassy in Paris, and received there (from date stamp) on 3 May 1952, contained in ibid.

13. A typed letter, dated 7 May 1952, from the British Embassy, consular section, Paris to the Claims Department of the Foreign Office, London, contained in ibid.

14. A typed letter, dated 24 June 1952, from the Foreign Office to the consular section of the British embassy, Paris, contained in ibid.

15. A letter marked 'secret and personal', dated 18 May 1951, to Sir Ralph Stevenson GCMG in Cairo from the Foreign Office, contained in Foreign Office records, FO 141/1499, The National Archives, Kew.

16. A typed despatch marked 'Secret, Personal', dated 12 May 1951, entitled 'draft letter to Mr Bowker from H.E.', and attached to reply-telegram (referred to in note 114) in the same file, contained in Foreign Office records, FO 141/1499, The National Archives, Kew.

7. THE QUESTION OF THE SUCCESSION TO THE IMAMATE (1953–1958)

1. A typed note marked 'Personal' from Sir G. Laithwaite to Mr D. Dodds-Parker, dated 14.6.1955, contained in ibid.

2. A copy of a note dated 15 June 1955, from Douglas Dodds-Parker to Major C.E. Mott-Radclyffe MP, contained in ibid.

3. A short report dated 19 June 1939, sent by T. Hickinbotham of the British Consulate and Political Agency, Muscat to the Hon'ble Lt Col Sir Trenchard Fowle KCIE CBE, Political Resident in the Persian Gulf, Bushire, added (as a copy) to a letter from T. Fowle to Sir Aubrey Metcalfe KCIE CSI MVO, Secretary to the Government of India, External Affairs Department, and contained in India Office Records, op. cit.

4. A file marked 'Secret' from the East Africa department of the Colonial Office, entitled 'Status of the Aga Khan and Succession to the Title: part I'. The file period is 1954–1956, and a marker stating 'Closed until 1991' is attached to the front cover. In Colonial Office records, CO 822/746, The National Archives, Kew.

5. A typed draft letter with a handwritten addition, dated 13 February 1955 from Mr Antrobus at the Foreign Office to K.W. Blaxter Esq CMG at the Colonial Office, contained in ibid.

6. A typed note, dated by hand 12/2/1955, and from unidentified author(s), attached to ibid.

7. A file marked 'Secret' from the East Africa department of the Colonial Office, entitled 'Status of the Aga Khan and succession to the Title: part II'. The file period is 1957–1959, and markers stating 'Closed until 2008' and 'Safe Room 2740' are attached to the front cover. The word '2008' is crossed out, and a penned word 'Released' is substituted. In Colonial Office records, CO 822/1209, The National Archives, Kew.

8. A typed noted from Mr Kisch at the Colonial Office to Mr King (department not identified) dated 14 April 1955, contained in ibid.

9. A typed note, signature illegible, dated 24 June 1955, contained in ibid.

10. Copy of a typed note, marked 'SECRET—BY HAND' from Sir A.G. Allen to W.A.C. Mathieson Esq MBE at the Colonial Office, dated 27 July 1955, contained in ibid.

11. A typed note marked 'Secret' from Mr J.M. Kisch at the Colonial Office to J.P. Gibson Esq CBE at the Commonwealth Relations Office, dated 28 July 1955, contained in ibid.

12. A typed note, entitled 'Secret: Note dictated by H.H. Aga Khan to Sir A. George Allen on 19th July, 1955. (Copy No. 2)', contained in ibid.

13. A telegram, dated 11 July 1957, from Her Majesty's Consul-General in Geneva to the Foreign Office, contained in Foreign Office records, FO371/125627, The National Archives, Kew.

14. A typed note from Alan Lennox-Boyd, dated 12 July 1957, to the Prime Minister, as contained in ibid.

15. A written press statement by the Colonial Office information department, dated 15 July 1957, contained in ibid.

16. E. Waugh, *Black Mischief* (London 1932, new edition 2000).

17. Draft of a telegram sent from the Foreign Office to Geneva, marked 'En Clair', dated 12 July 1957, contained in Foreign Office records, op cit.

18. Letter, on personal stationery headed 'Barakat, Versoix-Geneva', dated 23 July 1957, from the Aga Khan (IV) to the Rt. Honourable Selwyn Lloyd CBE QC MP, Secretary of State for Foreign Affairs, London, contained in ibid.

19. A copy of a letter from The Rt. Honourable Selwyn Lloyd CBE QC MP, Secretary of State for Foreign Affairs, London, to Prince Karim Aga Khan, dated 29 July 1957, contained in ibid.

20. A draft letter, marked 'Confidential' and marked (by hand) 'Not to go', from Sir C. Dixon at the Commonwealth Relations Office to W.A.C. Mathieson Esq MBE at the Colonial Office, undated but (from the position in the files) written shortly after the death of Aga Khan III, contained in Dominions Office records, DO35/5260, The National Archives, Kew.

21. Copy of a memorandum, dated 18 July 1957, from Sir C. Dixon at the Commonwealth Relations Office to W.A.C. Mathieson Esq MBE at the Colonial Office, contained in ibid.

22. Outward telegram from the Commonwealth Relations Office, dated 2 August 1957, to the UK High Commissioners in India and Pakistan, contained in ibid.

23. A copy of a letter, with attachment, from Alan Lennox-Boyd to His High-ness the Aga Khan, dated 1 August 1957, contained in Foreign Office records, op cit.

24. A copy of the attachment to Ref. 138, from Alan Lennox-Boyd to His Highness the Aga Khan, dated 1 August 1957, contained in ibid.

25. A letter, dated 4 September 1957, and typed on personal stationery headed 'Yakymour, Le Cannet, Cannes', from the widow of Aga Khan III to Alan Lennox-Boyd, contained in Colonial Office records, CO 822/1209.

26. A copy of a letter dated 18 September 1957, to Mr D.L. Cole, MC, signature illegible, contained in Dominions Office records, op cit.

27. A copy of a letter dated 27 September 1957, from Alan Lennox-Boyd at the Foreign Office to H.H. The Begum Aga Khan, contained in ibid.

28. Copy of a letter dated 3 August 1957, sent from Kampala, Uganda, by Hassanali J. Hemani, Doctor of Watches, to Her Majesty The Queen, contained in Colonial Office records, CO 822/1209, The National Archives, Kew.

8. FIRMLY ESTABLISHED AS A FRIEND OF BRITAIN (1955–1969)

1. A file marked 'Levant department', dated 195%, and entitled 'Reports visit of Hassan Kassim Lakha, the Aga Khan's repre... 'ative, who is in Syria to organise the Ismaili community there', contained in Foreign Office records, FO 371/115974, The National Archives, Kew.

2. A letter marked 'confidential' and dated 23 March 1955, sent from the British Embassy, Damascus to the Levant Department at the Foreign Office, London, as contained in ibid.

3. A letter marked 'restricted' and dated 31 March 1955, sent from the British Embassy, Damascus, to the Commercial Relations and Export Department at the Board of Trade, London, as contained in ibid.

4. D. Douwes and M.N. Lewis, 'The Trials of the Syrian Isma'ilis in the First Decade of the 20th Century', *The International Journal of Middle East Studies* (1989).

5. File marked 'African department—Belgian Congo', dated 1955, and entitled 'Followers of the Aga Khan', as contained in Foreign Office records, FO 371/113571, The National Archives, Kew.

6. Letter marked 'Confidential' and dated 18 May 1955, to T.E. Bromley Esq at the Foreign Office, from Mr F.A.K. Harrison at the Commonwealth Relations Office, contained in ibid.

7. Letter dated 16 July 1955, to T.E. Bromley Esq CMG at the Foreign Office, from W.A.C. Mathieson at the Colonial Office, contained in ibid.

8. File marked 'Confidential', dated 1957–1959, and entitled 'Proposal for Ismaili Community in South Africa to move to East Africa', contained in Colonial Office records, CO 822/1211, The National Archives, Kew.

9. Draft letter, dated 8 July 1958, from Alan Lennox-Boyd at the Colonial Office to the Rt. Hon. The Earl of Home at the Commonwealth Relations Office, contained in ibid.

10. Letter dated 14 July 1958, from the Earl of Home at the Commonwealth Relations Office to Alan Lennox-Boyd at the Colonial Office, contained in ibid.

11. Letter dated 19 August 1958 from Aga Khan IV to Alan Lennox-Boyd at the Colonial Office, contained in ibid.

12. File marked 'Confidential', dated 1957–1959, and entitled 'Proposal for Ismaili Community in South Africa to move to East Africa', contained in Colonial Office records, CO 822/1211, The National Archives, Kew.

13. Letter dated 16 October 1958 from W.L. Gorell Barnes at the Colonial Office to Sir Richard Turnbull KCMG, Governor of Tanganyika, contained in Colonial Office records, op cit.

14. A letter marked 'Confidential', dated 17 November 1958 and headed Office of the Chief Secretary, Private Bag, Dar es Salaam, from A.J. Grattan-Bellew to W.L Gorell Barnes Esq CB CMG at the Colonial Office, contained in Colonial Office records ibid.

15. Internal Colonial Office memo, dated 25 November 1958, addressed to Mr Rolfe and Mr Webber from a Mr K.G. Fry, op cit.

16. A letter marked 'Confidential and Personal', dated 12 December 1958, from W.L. Gorell Barnes at the Colonial Office to Sir Evelyn Baring GCMG KCVO, Governor of Kenya, contained in Colonial Office records, op cit.

17. A letter dated 24 March 1959, from Alan Lennox-Boyd at the Colonial Office to His Highness the Aga Khan, contained in ibid.

18. A letter dated 17 March 1959, from the Aga Khan to Alan Lennox-Boyd at the Colonial Office, contained in ibid.

19. A despatch dated 10 April 1959, from Alan Lennox-Boyd at the Colonial Office to His Highness the Aga Khan, contained in ibid.

20. A brief description of the role of Aga Khan I and II in Nizari Ismaili history, as represented on the Institute of Ismaili Studies website (London 2006).

21. A file marked 'Political Agency, Kuwait', and entitled 'Visit of Prince Sadruddin Aga Khan to Gulf on behalf of High Commissioner for Refugee[s]', as contained in Foreign Office archives, FO 371/153685, The National Archives, Kew.

22. A copy of an unsigned letter, dated 9 July 1960, from H.M. Political Agency, Kuwait to the British Residency, Bahrain, in ibid.

23. A copy of an unsigned letter, dated 11 September 1960, from H.M. Political Agency, Kuwait to the British Residency, Bahrain, in ibid.

24. File entitled 'Future of the Ismaili community in Uganda', as contained in Dominions Office records, DO 35/5260, The National Archives, Kew; File entitled 'Future of the Ismaili community in Uganda', contained in the Constitutional Department of the Dominions Office records, DO 35/8075, The National Archives, Kew. Undated.

25. Inward telegram, marked 'Cypher priority' and 'Secret', dated 30 September 1960, from 'Karachi' to the Commonwealth Relations Office, and allocated to the Constitutional Department, contained in ibid.

26. An outward telegram, marked 'Cypher, Priority' and 'Secret', dated 21 October 1960, from the Commonwealth Relations Office to 'Karachi', contained in Dominions Office records (n. 173).

27. A file entitled 'Cancer Research at the Aga Khan Hospital, Kenya', contained in Colonial Office records, CO 822/3064, The National Archives, Kew.

28. Letter, dated 12 February 1963 and headed 'Chalet Darannour, Gstaad, O.B., Switzerland', from His Highness Aga Khan IV to the Rt. Hon. Duncan Sandys M.P. at the Commonwealth Relations Office, Downing Street, London, contained in ibid.

29. Memorandum dated 14 March 1963, marked 'Confidential' and headed 'Council of Ministers; The Aga Khan Platinum Jubilee Hospital Nairobi; Proposed Capital Grant; Memorandum by the Deputy Governor', contained in ibid.

30. A file entitled 'Passports, facilities for minors; stateless Ismaili children', and marked 'Confidential, closed until 2000', contained in Foreign and Commonwealth Office records, FCO 53/76, The National Archives, Kew.

31. A typed memorandum, marked 'Confidential' and dated 5 March 1969, from Sir Edward Peck KCMG of the Foreign and Commonwealth Office, addressed to Mr Mason and copied to the East African Department, the Arabian Department, the South Asian Department and the British Embassy, Paris, contained in ibid.

32. A typed memorandum, marked 'Confidential' and dated 19 September 1969, from Sir Edward Peck of the Foreign and Colonial Office, addressed to, among others, the East African Department, the South Asian Department and the British Embassies in Paris, Kinshasa, Nairobi and Kuwait, contained in ibid.

33. A copy of a letter, marked 'Confidential' and dated 25 September 1969, from Miss T.M. Cullis of the Nationality and Treaty Division of the Foreign and Commonwealth Office, addressed to Mr W.M. Lee of the Nationality Division of the Home Office, contained in ibid.

34. Memo dated 8 October 1969 from L.E. Webb of the Nationality and Treaty Department to Sir Edward Peck, both of the Foreign and Commonwealth Office, contained in ibid.

35. A handwritten letter, dated 20 October 1969 and headed 'Rue des Ursins, Paris IV' from H.H. the Aga Khan (IV) to 'Sir Edward' (presumably Sir Edward Peck KCMG of the Foreign and Commonwealth Office), contained in ibid.

BIBLIOGRAPHY

Official records of the Ministry of Agriculture, Fisheries and Foods, as deposited in The National Archives, Kew

File MAF 121/148   Containing miscellaneous correspondence of the Ministry of Agriculture, Fisheries and Food.

Official records of the British Delegation to the multinational conference regarding the peace settlement concluding the First World War, as deposited in The National Archives, Kew

File RO 608/272   Entitled *Views of the Aga Khan on proposed Turkish settlement*, dated 1920.

BIBLIOGRAPHY CONCERNING THE ORIGINS, HISTORY, DEVELOPMENT AND DOCTRINES OF THE ISMAILI MOVEMENT

Algar, H., 'The Revolt of Aga Khan Mahalatti and the Transference of the Ismai'ili Imamate to India', *Studia Islamica*, Paris 1969.

Aziz, K.K. (ed.), *Selected Speeches and Writings of Sir Sultan Muhammad Shah*, London 1998.

Badakhchani, S.J. (ed.), *Paradise of Submission: A Medieval Treatise on Ismaili. Thought. A New Persian Edition and English Translation of Nasir al-Din Tusi's Rawda-yi Taslim*, London 2005.

Clarke, P.B., 'The Ismailis: A Study of Community', *The British Journal of Sociology*, London 1976.

Daftary, F., *The Ismailis: Their History and Doctrines*, Cambridge 1990.

———, *Mediaeval Ismaili History and Thought*, Cambridge 1996.

———, *The Assassin Legends: Myths of the Ismailis*, London 2001.

———, *Ismailis in Medieval Muslim Societies*, London and New York 2005.

Douwes, D. and M.N. Lewis, 'The Trials of the Syrian Isma'ilis in the First Decade of the 20th Century', *The International Journal of Middle East Studies* (1989).

Hopkirk, P., *Setting the East Ablaze: Lenin's Dream of an Empire in Asia*, New York and London, 1984.

———, *On Secret Service East of Constantinople: The Plot to Bring down the British Empire*, London 1994.

———, *The Great Game*, London 2006.

Khan, D.S., *Crossing the Threshold: Understanding Religious Identities in South*, London 2005.

Kepel, G., *The War for Muslim Minds: Islam and the West*, Harvard 2004.

Lewis, B., *The Assassins: A Radical Sect in Islam*, London 1967.

Massie, R.K., *Dreadnought: Britain, Germany and the Coming of the First World War*, New York 2003.

———, *Castles of Steel: Britain, Germany and the Winning of the Great War*, New York 1998.

Meherally, A., *A History of the Agakhani Ismailis*, Burnaby (Can.) 1991.

BIBLIOGRAPHY

Nanji, A., 'Modernization and Change in the Ismaili Community in East Africa: A Perspective', *Journal of Religion in Africa*, 1974.

Sobhani, Ayatollah J., *Doctrines of Shi'i Islam: A Compendium of Imami Beliefs and Practices*, London 2001.

Taji-Farouki, S. and B.M. Nafi (eds), *Islamic Thought in the Twentieth Century*, London 2004.

Waugh, E., *Black Mischief*, London 1932 (ed. 2000).

Willey, P., *Eagle's Nest: Ismaili Castles in Iran and Syria*, London and New York 1998.

SELECT BIBLIOGRAPHY ON THE SOCIOLOGY OF RELIGION, AND THE SOCIOLOGY OF CHANGE.

Chryssides, G.D., *New Religious Movements—some Problems of Definition*, as published on the religionswissenschaft website of the University of Marburg, accessed June 2007.

Deutsch, K., *Nationalism and Social Communication*, Harvard 1966.

Gladwell, M., *The Tipping Point*, New York 2000 (included the theories of M. Granovetter as used in the book).

Stark, R. and W.S. Bainbridge, *A Theory of Religion*, New York 1987.

APPENDICES

A CHRONOLOGY OF THE LIFE OF HIS HIGHNESS SIR SULTAN MUHAMMAD SHAH GCSI GCMG GCIE GCVO, AGA KHAN III (1877–1957)

1877	Born in Karachi, British India.
1885	Death of Aga Khan II, and succession to the Imamate. Commences education at Eton College, progressing to Cambridge University thereafter.
1896	Marries Shazadi Begum, first cousin and granddaughter of Aga Khan I.
1897	Received by Queen Victoria, and knighted KCIE.
1902	Appointed member of the Imperial Legislative Council, as youngest ever member; knighted GCIE by King Edward VII.
1906	Leads Muslim delegation to Simla, demanding a separate Muslim electorate. Elected president of the All India Muslim League.
1908	Marries ('*muta*' marriage) C.T. Magliono, a ballet dancer.
1912	Knighted GCIE by King George V.
1914	Provides active support to the British Empire during the First World War.
1916	Raised to the dignity of First Class Ruling Prince in the Presidency of Bombay by British Government.
1923	Regularises marriage to Miss Magliono.
1924	Nominated for Nobel Peace Prize for work on Turkish-Allied peace agreement.
1928	President of the Indian All Parties Muslim Conference.
1929	Marries Andrée Josephine Carron.

1930–1932	Leads delegation of Indian Muslims to Round Table conferences.
1934	Appointed member of the Privy Council.
1937	Elected president of the League of Nations.
1943	Divorces Josephine Carron.
1944	Marries Yvonne Labrousse, his social secretary.
1954	Health deteriorates; largely withdraws from public life.
1957	Dies in Switzerland; entombed in Aswan, Egypt.

A REPORT FROM THE GOVERNOR OF TANGANYIKA
CONCERNING THE FUNERAL OF AGA KHAN III AT ASWAN, UPPER
EGYPT, AND AN ACKNOWLEDGEMENT FROM JOHN PROFUMO,
THEN PARLIAMENTARY UNDERSECRETARY FOR THE COLONIES
(BOTH DOCUMENTS AS CONTAINED IN COLONIAL OFFICE
RECORDS, CO 822/1209, THE NATIONAL ARCHIVES, KEW)

Enclosure to a despatch addressed to the Rt.Hon. Alan. T. Lennox-Boyd, M.P., Secretary of State for the Colonies, from Sir Edward Twining, Governor of Tanganyika as Her Majesty's Government Representative at the Obsequies of the late Aga Khan.

[Text begins] I was on safari and ungetatable [sic, MvG] when the Secretary of State's instructions for me to proceed to Aswan to represent the British Government at the burial of the late Aga Khan arrived. The following day, Saturday 13th July, I got the message and returning to Dar-es-Salaam found that while every possible effort was being made to sort the situation out, there was little information about when the burial was to take place, or how one could get to Aswan. It was thought that the burial was to have been on the 16th July, but fortunately this was changed to Friday, 19th July.

The obvious way to fly to Cairo and take the train to Aswan, but it was impossible to get a passage on one of the few aeroplanes that now land in Cairo. I, therefore, decided to attach myself to the Ismaili delegation who had chartered an East African Airways Dakota. In order to enable me to fulfil certain engagements on the morning of Wednesday, 17th July, I accompanied by my Private Secretary, Mr J.W.D. Margetson, took the Government aeroplane to Nairobi, changed to a scheduled service of Alitalia to Khartoum, arriving there at midnight where I was met by the Charge d'Affaires, Mr Walker, and the Private Secretary to the Prime Minister. Early the next morning I joined the Ismaili Dakota and we set off for Wadi Half where we refuled. [sic, MvG]

Permission for us to land at Aswan was refused on the grounds that there were no Customs, but according to general gossip, it was because the Israelis had threatened to bomb the Aswan dam and there was, therefore, a force of 'Mig' fighters stationed as Aswan. We were told we could land at Luxor, provided we took a course well away from Aswan.

We arrived at Luxor at about 2 p.m. and spent an uncomfortable three hours at the Airport lounge while Egyptian bureaucracy decided what to do with twenty-nine British subjects who had descended upon them almost unannounced, without visas, with little currency, except sterling Travellers Cheques which were unacceptable, and with an apparent determination to break every bureaucratic rule which they so cherished. After an immense amount of wrangling and telephoning to Cairo, nothing happened, except that we sweltered in a temperature of 114°F. However, one of the Ismaili leaders started to seek all the passengers, and by a strange coincidence about a quarter of an hour later a telephone message was received from Cairo giving us clearance; a bus arrived and we were all allowed to go to the Luxor Hotel.

The Ismaili leaders then tried to hire a bus to take us through by road, a journey of eight hours, but as the owner appeared to think that we wanted to buy the bus from the amount he was to charge, and we learned that the road was out of order, this had to be abandoned. Undaunted, they chartered two second-class railway carriages which they hoped to hook on to an express train, but this was not allowed and they began to look for an engine. Having located one, there was wrangling about the price which was £225. Having no money and the bank refusing to cash our cheques, we seemed to be in a dilemma. However, the leaders raised the money from some Muslims and naively told me this showed the advantages of being members of the Muslim Brotherhood. I had to warn them not to use this phrase as the Muslim Brotherhood in Egypt was a proscribed society.

We had a prolonged wait on the railway station from about midnight until 3 a.m., being told that it was unlikely that we could leave until 5 a.m. as it was a single line and a train was coming the other way. This would not have enable us to have reached Aswan in time for the ceremony. By a miracle at 3.15 p.m. a gleaming white special train of Wagon Lits and dining cars turned up from Cairo, apparently unbeknownst to the Station Master or the signal man. It had been chartered by the Pakistani Ismailis, and without further ado, we transferred to the train and made the journey to Aswan, I in the comparative luxury of a filthy, dirty coupe sleeping car of very ancient vintage.

We had an hour to spare before the ceremony on arrival, but we soon learned from Prince Sadrudin, who met me, that it had been postponed until 4 o'clock in the afternoon (the hottest time of day). So we went to the Cataract Hotel which had been specially opened for the occasion. It is a huge pile in the Edwardian Egyptian sytle [sic, author] with a decor which can only be described as a mixture between a Turkish Bath and the Alambra Theatre. I arranged to pay a formal visit to the new Aga Khan and took the opportunity of conveying the condolences of the British, Tanganyika and East African Governments and our congratulations on his succession. The young man asked us to sit down and have a nice little talk, but his father, uncle and brother all came into the room and we had a somewhat uproarious conversation for about half-an-hour on horse racing, American universities and Tanganyika politics.

The rest of the morning was spent sweltering on the verandah of the hotel in a temperature of 120°F. I was pestered by more than thirty newspaper men; the Egyptians all tired to get me to say that I had been abominably treated, but I made it clear that my treatment had been absolutely correct and I had no complaints.

We had lunch with the four Princes and immediately afterwards met the Governor of Aswan who took us to his launch on which we crossed the Nile. I had brought with me my morning coat and top hat with which always goes my umbrella, but fortunately I was spared having to wear it and a tropical suit was sufficiently formal. I took by umbrella, however, as an emblem of my respectability, and extremely convenient it was either to use as a stick when negotiating the slippery steep paths on the banks of the Nile, or to shade me and as many others as could get near it, from the scorching rays of the sun.

The burial ceremony took place in an architecturally tasteless villa which belonged to the late Aga Khan. The coffined body was in the dining-room which led out into the drawing room which again led out onto a courtyard where a marble tomb had been erected. Some fifty women had been waiting round the coffin since 11 o'clock in the morning and were now joined by between 400 and 500 men. Every window was hermetically sealed and with the stifling heat and the human humidity, the conditions were most uncomfortable, especially as chaos prevailed and there was not room for more than 150 to 200 people to be there in any comfort.

At length the Begum appeared, supported by two attendants: a dignified but tragic figure who sat on a sort of tugget and sprawled on the coffin in paroxysms of tears and grief. When she had finished, a Sheikh and then the new Aga Khan recited prayers. Aly Khan sat on the coffin and knocked three times with his ear to the keyhole. He then drew the key from his pocket and locked the panel. The coffin was borne to the tom on the shoulders of the four princes and two other officials. It was very heavy and Aly Khan, who was obviously not in training for such exertions, kept on shouting out that he could not go any further.

When they at last got to the tomb, the Egyptian Governor took over the so-called arrangements, and having roped the coffin up, nobody know how to get it into the tomb. The Begum, with great self-possession, sent for the man she called "the specialist" who brought in some pieces of timber to which it was attached. After a long delay and much shouting, it was lifted and lowered into the tomb. But alas! The tomb was too small to receive it, so it had to be moved back again. Some masons were sent for who had to knock part of the tomb away which took about half an hour. The Governor of Aswan got very excited and asked whether it really mattered because they would have to undo it all the next day and take the coffin out again and put it back properly and why could they not leave it as it was, and so on. Finally, the tomb had been made large enough and the coffin was lowered into it, but not very straightly.

Thinking that this was the last part of the ceremony, I left the courtyard to recover my shoes which I had been made to take off, and I was enjoying the shade of my umbrella whilst a huge marble slab was taken in and afixed. I was then sent for by the Begum to whom I gave my condolences. Despite the chaotic arrangements, the devotion of the Ismailis was very moving and they were all obviously sincerely griefstricken. But as usual on these sort of occasions, the whole ceremony was completely marred by the impossible behaviour of the Press correspondents who, without regard to anybody's feelings or any sense of decency, ruined the ceremony by taking flashlight photographs continuously. I understand that on the previous day they had behaved even worse when the coffin was received at the villa, and Aly Khan had used physical violence against some of them.

We then returned to the Nile and boarded the Governor of Aswan's launch. Not only did the V.I.Ps—i.e. the family, the Governor of Aswan, the Pakistani Ambassador from Cairo and the Governor of Tanganyika come on board, but about eighty other people, and the Governor of Aswan kept on shouting and gesticulating that the launch was about to sink. However, we reached the other bank in one piece and having drunk the residual stock of mineral waters which the hotel possessed, we said "goodbye" to Aly Khan, Sadruddin and Aymin, the Ambassador and the Governor of Aswan. The last named had been out of his way to be cordial to me to which I responded to the extent that the heat allowed.

We left Aswan in the same train at 10.30 p.m., arriving at Luxor a little before 3 a.m. After two hours rest we went to the aerodrome, found out aeroplane intact and set off on the return journey which was eventless, apart from one of the lady Ismaili passengers having a heart attack.

Meanwhile, at Luxor the pilot and steward, being in possession of British passports, were confined to the hotel by the Police. They managed, however, to steal the guard's Patchet gun and ammunition and took him to the airport where thy filled him up with beer in the aeroplane while the pilot—illegally no doubt—contacted Nairobi by radio and arranged with Cairo for the payment of £150 which was due before we were allowed to take off. They then returned to the hotel where the guard was thankful to have his gun given back to him.

The journey was a most exhausting one, incredibly uncomfortable, worsened by the anxieties as to the uncertainties of the next move and suffered in an intolerable heat, but it did show up magnificently the qualities of the Ismaili delegation whose leaders showed a superb sense of determination and who bulldozed their way through every difficulty regardless of cost or consequence and invariably came out on top. They treated me with the utmost kindness and attention and, indeed, they and all the other delegations from Singapore, Burma, India, Pakistan, Iraq, East Africa, Madagascar, Belgian Congo, Portuguese East Africa and the Union of South Africa went out of their way to tell me how much they appreciated her Majesty's Government having done the honour of sending a special representative, and how glad they were that it was a person who was so closely associated with one of their communities.

I shall be submitting a claim from the Tanganyika Government for the expenses involved in the journey. It will be impossible to give a full account because of the curious ways in which we had to finance it. Moreover, the Tanganyika delegation asked me to regard myself as their guest. Although in normal circumstances this would not be desirable, I think that it would hurt their feelings if we did not accept the hospitality at the hotels and on the train, and in any case it would be quite impossible to make any assessment of the proportion which I drank of the enormous quantities of Evian, Vichy, Perrier, San Pellegrino, soda water, fizzy lemonade and other concoctions which were ordered and consumed until all stocks were exhausted wherever we went. Nor shall I claim my contribution to the collection taken at the Luxor Airport to which I have already referred.—Government House, Dar-es-Salaam, 23rd July, 1957.

To which the following answer and acknowledgement was sent by John Profumo, then Parliamentary Undersecretary for the Colonies:

Colonial Office, the Church House, Great Smith Street, London S.W.1, 12 August, 1957. [Text begins.] Sir, I have the honour to acknowledge the receipt of your despatch No. 666 of the 26th July and to thank you for your absorbing account of the journey to Aswan and the funeral of the late Aga Khan. [...] I am sincerely grateful to you for so readily agreeing to undertake this uncertain assignment and for surmounting with such good humour the discomforts and perplexing situations with which it proved fraught. You will wish to know that His Highness Karim Aga Khan has written to the Foreign Secretary expressing his gratitude for your attendance at the obsequies of his grandfather.[...] I have the honour to be, Sir, Your most obedient, humble servant, John Profumo.

A CHRONOLOGY OF THE LIFE OF HIS HIGHNESS AGA KHAN IV (1936—PRESENT)

1936   Born in Geneva; son of prince Aly Khan, grandson of Aga Khan III.

1957   Succeeds to the Imamate as Aga Khan IV; granted the dignity of 'Highness' by Queen Elizabeth II.

1959   Graduated with BA (Hons) in Islamic history from Harvard University; granted the title of 'Royal Highness' by the Shah of Persia.

1969	Marries Sarah Frances Croker-Poole, a divorcee and former model.
1977	Founds the Institute of Ismaili Studies, London.
1994	Divorces.
1998	Marries Dr Gabriele Princess of Leiningen (*née* Gabriële Thyssen).
2004	Seeks divorce.
2005	Receives the Andrew Carnegie medal for Philanthropy; receives honorary Companionship of the Order of Canada.

LIST OF ABBREVIATIONS REGARDING THE BRITISH HONOURS OF AGA KHAN III

KCIE	Knight Commander of the Indian Empire (British Indian).
GCIE	Knight Grand Commander of the Indian Empire (British Indian).
GCSI	Knight Grand Commander of the Star of India (British Indian).
GCMG	Knight Grand Cross of the Order of St Michael & St George (British).
GCVO	Knight Grand Cross of the Royal Victorian Order (British).

A NOTE ON THE SPELLING AND PUNCTUATION IN THE MAIN TEXT, THE REPRESENTATION OF QUOTATIONS, AND THE METHOD OF REFERENCING

In the main text, contemporary British English spelling is used. Where quotations are made from official British archives, these texts are transposed literally, including any mistakes in grammar, punctuation or spelling. These may be indicated by '[sic, MvG]' if it is deemed that these mistakes may confuse the reader. Where documents are typed, but signed by hand, the handwritten signature is preceded by the notification (Sgd.). Where signatures or text are illegible, this is specifically mentioned in the quotation. Where underlining or crossing out of individual words or (parts of) sentences took place in the original text, this is transposed to the quotation in the narrative. The same applies to the spelling of the words 'Muslim' or 'Mohammedan' which appear in many varieties in the British official correspondence. In quotation from publications other than British official archives, the literal text is transposed from the publication as it appeared in the version which is referenced.

Where documents are referenced, this is indicated by a superscript footnote reference. The footnotes are contained and elaborated on in chapter 12. For official archival documents originating from either The National Archives at Kew or the British Library in London, the reference number of the file from which the document was recovered is referenced, thereby enabling retrieval and cross-verification. For documents such as reference works, collected writings and speeches and such like, the specific edition from which the text is quoted is described. In the rare cases where a document does not contain a specific date, an inferred date (or a wider time period during which it is likely to have emanated) is mentioned, as derived either from the position in the file relative to other documents, or from the fact that it is referred to in other documents which do have an exact dating.

Outside the above specifics, the presentation of the text is based as far as practicable on *New Hart's Rules: the Handbook of Style for Writers and Editors*, Oxford 2005.

A DEFINITION OF THE TERM 'ISMAILI' AS USED IN THE BOOK

Except where explicitly mentioned (which is exclusively in chapter 2), the term 'Ismaili' as used in the text refers to the Nizari Ismaili movement, which forms part of the overall Shi'a Imami tradition. Given the fact that today's major Nizari Ismaili institutions (such as the Institute of Ismaili Studies in London) refer to themselves as 'Ismaili', the same descriptive term is used in the which deals with the period 1840 to 1966. A similar logic is followed in the British official correspondence which is referenced in the narrative. On occasion, British officials used the term 'Khojas' when describing the Nizari Ismailis. Technically, this is incorrect since this only refers to those Ismailis of Indian ethnicity, who were converted from Hinduism to the Nizari Ismaili interpretation of Islam. Nevertheless, this term is on occasions used when quoting from official British sources.

Other Muslim movements which may lay claim to being described as Ismaili and indeed have Shi'a Imami traditions are mentioned in chapter 2 for reasons of historical context, but these play no further role in the narrative as their subsequent development falls outside the scope of the research described herein.

INDEX

INDEX